Luke: Part 1

A Study of Luke 1–8

By Hope A. Blanton and Christine B. Gordon

19Baskets

Luke: Part 1
A Study of Luke 1–8
© 2019 by Hope A. Blanton and Christine B. Gordon
ISBN 978-1-946862-10-5

19Baskets, Inc.
PO Box 31291
Omaha, NE 68131
https://19baskets.com

First Edition

Cover design by Sophie Calhoun

Photography by Michael Gordon

Endorsements

"Hope Blanton and Chris Gordon have once again provided the church with a rich yet accessible resource in this study on Luke's Gospel. They have a gift for bringing the historical context to life, making the scenes we encounter in Luke come alive in new ways. Their obvious love of God's Word is contagious, and you will not only delight in studying his Word; you will be better equipped for further study because they show us how to study. Ultimately, though, this is a study that will lead you to Jesus, let you encounter him afresh, and ask you to respond to his claims, his life, and his love."

— **Courtney Doctor**, coordinator for women's training and content, the Gospel Coalition, speaker, Bible teacher, and author of *From Garden to Glory: A Bible Study on the Bible's Story*

"Whether you're a new believer, college student, young mom, seasoned mentor, or Bible study leader, I can not recommend the At His Feet Studies highly enough! At His Feet Studies make deep and intentional Bible study approachable for women in various seasons of their walk with the Lord. This study on Luke guides the reader through observation, interpretation, and application in a helpful and accessible way, even for a mama of young children, like me! I find myself walking away with fresh insight and practical truths to apply to my daily life."

— **Hunter Beless**, host of Journeywomen Podcast

"I hear from young moms all the time who believe that in-depth Bible study isn't an option for them because they are in an intense season with limited time and mental energy. This study is a gift to those women. Chris and Hope offer a gift wrapped twenty-minute daily experience that will leave women not only with a deeper knowledge of the book of Luke but more enthralled with the person of Jesus and more aware of how he is at work in, through, and around them. This study raises the bar for women's ministry tools by demonstrating that limited time and mental energy do not mean that we must bypass in-depth study to obtain the application points we crave. Chris and Hope offer a Christ-exalting resource that meets busy women where we are and allows us to see him as he is."

— **Abbey Wedgeworth**, Gentle Leading

"This study gives one time to pause, to be reminded, and to be made certain of what you can know to be true about the humanity and divinity of Jesus. Study Luke's account alone, or in a group, through the commentaries and questions written by Chris and Hope and know that the kingdom of heaven is at hand!"

— **Betty McCracken**, Bible teacher of forty years

Contents

At His Feet Story

A few years ago, Hope started looking for materials for the women's fall Bible study at our church. While she found a great number of quality Bible studies, she had a hard time finding studies written for women by women who were reformed. She also had a tough time finding in-depth studies of the Scripture that didn't take a whole lot of time. In a moment of desperation, Hope asked Chris if she would be willing to co-write a study on Romans, convincing her by asking, "I mean, really, how hard could it be?" And so it began. Weekly emails back and forth, Chris deep in commentaries, Hope mulling over questions, tweaking, editing, asking, pondering. A group of women at Redeemer Presbyterian Church in Lincoln, Nebraska, patiently bore with us as we experimented with them every week and learned to find our rhythm as writers.

Two years later, Hope approached Chris again, softening her up by telling her she could choose any book she wanted. 1 Samuel it was. Old Testament narrative is the best. Another study was born. About this time, women started asking us for copies of the two studies we had written. While trying to send endless pdfs to people around the country via email, a pastor friend who happens to be a publisher approached Chris and Hope at a party, offering to publish the Bible studies. Suddenly, we had a way to get these into the hands of women who could use them. This had been the point of the whole enterprise – to help make the book of Romans accessible to women. But what would the name be?

During the first century, when Jesus walked the earth, a Jewish rabbi would have been surrounded by his students, with some of the men sitting as his feet to learn and listen. This was the custom, the understood norm of the day. But in Luke 10:39, Mary sat at the feet of Jesus. Mary, a woman, was taught by this unconventional

1

rabbi. Mary was given the dignity of taking in his words, his pauses, his tone. To Jesus, she was every bit as worthy of his teaching as the men in the room were—and so are we, his women students today. And so we are At His Feet Bible Studies, hoping to sit at the feet of Jesus while we study his Word.

Please find our other available studies at our website:
www.athisfeetonline.com

User Guide

There is no right way to lead a Bible study. Every Bible study group is made up of different types of women with various sets of needs and dynamics. Below are some suggestions that might be helpful when using At His Feet Studies. Read it through. Use what you want. Forget the rest. We're glad you're here.

Participants Guide

This study is laid out like most commentaries. Each chapter is broken up into smaller portions with explanations of the verses in order. There are questions in the chapters before and after the commentary. The first set of questions are Observation Questions designed to help the reader interact with the basic content of the chapter. The second set of questions are Reflection Questions designed to help the reader engage her heart with the text in a vulnerable way.

Start by reading the Scripture passage noted at the top of the study page. Then answer the Observation Questions. Next, go back and read the Scripture side by side with the commentary, pausing between each grouping of verses to absorb both the commentary and the text more deeply. Then move on to answer the Reflection Questions.

Leaders Guide

There are eight questions for each study. When in a group setting, we suggest choosing your favorite Reflection Questions to focus on, especially if you run short on time. If you have more time feel free to work through all the questions. For those groups where people have not had the time and space to read through the commentary and questions, you can simply read the commentary out loud at the beginning of your time. That way all women can participate. We always suggest reading the Scripture passage out loud before you begin.

Extras

The focus verse is something to spend time reflecting on since it's the heart of the passage. Consider memorizing it individually or as a group.

Use the section we have labeled "Reflections, Curiosities, Frustrations" to write down things about the text that seem confusing to you or hard for you to wrap your brain around. This is meant to give you space to express how you're a work in progress as you work through this text and engage with God's Word.

Study 1

Introduction to the Gospel of Luke

At some point in our lives, most of us have read or listened to some or all of the Gospel of Luke. Maybe you recited the birth announcement to the shepherds in a Christmas pageant as a child. Maybe you've seen verses painted on crafty banners for sale. Maybe you've studied the entire Book of Luke. It can be tempting to gloss over familiar passages like many we find in Luke's Gospel. We've heard them before. We could recite parts of them. We already know the story.

But how well do you know the one in the story? When was the last time you came face to face with the Jesus of the Gospels and were in awe? When was the last time his actions took your breath away? Have his words shocked you lately? Have his commands prompted your repentance? Have his promises made your heart long with hope? It is our hearts that grow dull, not his story. He is just as vibrant and alive as our souls ache for him to be. As you meet him afresh in his Word, pray that his Spirit would attend your reading and give you ears to hear. You will find him wildly captivating, unceasingly lovely.

Before diving into the text, a few observations and comments will help us prepare.

Who was Luke anyway? It may seem strange at first to read a book by someone who isn't even mentioned in the Bible until Paul speaks of him in Colossians 4:14 as "the beloved physician." But Luke was no stranger to the story of Jesus's life. He was a traveling companion of Paul and was imprisoned with him for two years in

Caesarea. Both the "we" sections of Acts and hundreds of years of tradition confirm for us that Luke and Paul spent much time together.

But Luke was not the typical biblical author. For starters, he was a Gentile, meaning he was not Jewish. He never met Jesus but was converted by the early church. Luke lived in the first century AD and probably wrote his Gospel between 60 and 70 AD. He was clearly an educated man, as his Gospel's prologue (Luke 1:1-4) was written in classical Greek, probably the best Greek in the New Testament. In chapter 1, verse 5, he switches to koine Greek, the common Greek language of his day.

How is Luke's Gospel different from those of Matthew, Mark, and John? First, Luke's is the longest of the Gospels, and it is the only one with a sequel—the Book of Acts. Luke and Acts together make up more than one quarter of the entire New Testament. Clearly God gave this man a large amount of influence. Second, Luke sets his telling of the story of redemption firmly in the context of world history. He cites particular names and titles of rulers, geographical markers, and other datings to embed the life and ministry of Jesus in wider history. For example, in Luke 3:1-2, Luke cites six historical markers for the reader before he begins his narrative about John the Baptist. Luke is a careful historian, stating his desire to put together "an orderly account." He uses primary source material, including testimony of eyewitnesses. Some commentators think it entirely possible that he interviewed Mary for the birth narrative.

Third, Luke's Gospel is for everyone: Gentiles, women, the poor, the disreputable. Concerning the Gentiles: While Matthew writes his birth narrative beginning with Abraham, the father of the Jews (Matthew 1), Luke writes his birth narrative ending with Adam, the father of all humans. Concerning women: In the first eight chapters alone, Luke tells the birth story of Jesus from Mary's perspective, explains her encounter with Elizabeth, mentions Anna the prophetess, and tells the stories of raising the widow's son, the woman who anoints Jesus's feet with her hair, the woman in the crowd who is healed of her bleeding, and the women who are benefactors of and travel with Jesus. All of this in an age when most women were considered secondary and all Jewish men began their day with this prayer to God: "Thank you that you have not made me a Gentile, a slave, or a woman." Concerning the poor and disreputable: Luke points out the "unclean" people of society and Jesus's ministry to them multiple times. He explains that Jesus's birth announcement was to unclean shepherds. He highlights the way Jesus touches and heals lepers, the demon-possessed, and women. Luke is clearly painting a picture of salvation that is available for everyone, not just the Jews.

Why write a book about only Luke 1–8? Why not the whole book?

The Gospel of Luke has many parables and other accounts that aren't found in any of the other Gospels. Of course, we could do a survey and hit the highlights, but we have chosen a verse-by-verse treatment of the text. This allows us to settle into each scene, each parable, each interaction Jesus has. We want to experience the surprise Zechariah feels in the temple when the angel greets him. We want to sit in the crowd and marvel at Jesus's teaching in the sermon on the plain. We want to be at the table with Simon and Jesus when the ex-prostitute comes to wet Jesus's feet with her tears. These things are only possible if we go slowly through each chapter, noticing details and pointing out cultural and historical meanings.

This is the gospel for everyone. This is the story of redemption painted in vivid colors and shocking contrast. This is God inviting us, through his Son, into the glorious upside-down kingdom.

Reflection Questions

1. Have you ever read part or all of the Gospel of Luke? How would you describe the book?

2. Do you have a favorite passage from Luke? If so, which one?

3. Of all the information you read in the introduction, what did you learn that really stood out to you? Why?

4. What are you hoping studying Luke will do for your heart over the course of completing this Bible study?

Study 2

Angels and the Impossible

Read Luke 1:1-38

Observation Questions

1. Who wrote this account and why?

2. Who was Zechariah, and what happened to him?

3. Who was the angel that communicated to both Zechariah and Mary? How are the communications with each of them similar? How are they different?

Verses 1–4. Thousands would have known the story of Jesus's life and ministry. Luke had multiple written, eyewitness accounts. But the love and respect of a friend prompted him as he began to write what he calls "an orderly account." Theophilus, which means "lover of God," was probably not this friend's real name. The way Luke addresses him indicates that he was a person of rank, maybe a Roman officer. He may have even financed Luke's writing of the book. He had clearly been taught the faith, but he may or may not have been a believer. Luke, the systematic, careful doctor wanted to give his friend a methodically investigated narrative so that Theophilus might have certainty. Ultimately, Luke wanted his friend to be certain about who Jesus was. Of course, he was inspired and led by the Holy Spirit, but the Holy Spirit used the particular personality, place, and proclivities of Luke to capture this story both for Theophilus and for the billions that would read it after him. Through the meticulous work and loving intention of Luke the doctor, we enter the story of Jesus's life.

Verses 5–25. It was as if the stage had gone dark for a long, long time. In the drama of God revealing himself and his plan through the history of Israel, there was a drawn-out, silent intermission. No one heard from the God who had promised to rescue his people. There were no visions, no prophets, no word from Yahweh for over four hundred years. The ritual of offering sacrifices to God had continued. The temple still stood. The feasts of Israel, the Sabbaths, the telling of the stories of the Exodus went on. But it must have felt like the stories were all about the God of the past, not of the present. It must have felt like God had forgotten.

Enter Zechariah. Having been born in a line of priests, Zechariah would have had the responsibility of going to the temple in Jerusalem twice per year to perform whatever duty was chosen by lot. Because there were a limited number of tasks for the priests to carry out, burning the incense was an immense honor that a priest would perform only once in his life. For Zechariah, this would have been the high point of his existence. For just a few moments this man of God was to be as close to God as any human at the time could get. Burning incense symbolized the prayers of Israel going up to God. He and all of the worshippers waiting for him would have been praying for the salvation of Israel. Their prayers must have felt quite futile.

But our God is not a God who forgets. Zechariah may have given up praying for a child, but Zechariah's name means "the Lord has remembered." God had not forgotten his promise to bring a Messiah out of Israel. And in the darkness of the holy place, as Zechariah smelled the incense and waited before the Lord, he learned that God's remembering of Israel would include an individual remembrance of him. This is how our God works. He uses our stories, our losses, our longings, our voices, and our prayers to further his kingdom. When Zechariah voiced his doubt, the angel rebuked him. It is as if Zechariah was saying, "But I'm old," and the angel was saying, "But he's God." God is not limited by our limitations.

This is the first of countless glimpses of the upside-down kingdom in the Book of Luke. A barren woman was to have a child who would be a prophet like Elijah, the first in four hundred years. In Elizabeth's culture, not having any children meant extreme shame. God was about to take away her shame. Not only that, but in a crazy plot twist, God's first words to the world after centuries involved an infertile couple having a baby who would prepare the way for the savior of the world.

Verses 26-38. The scene changes from inside Jerusalem's temple to the countryside and a little town called Nazareth. Unlike today, where the majority of people are engaged to be married in their twenties and thirties, betrothal usually happened soon after puberty. Mary was probably in her early teens. Notice in verse 28 how the angel greets Mary. "Favored one" here is not a status Mary had earned. In Ephesians 1:6 this same Greek word is translated "blessed" or "freely given." Mary was not chosen because she did something right. God gave her this honor in the same way he gives all believers honor—"apart from any merit of their own." Unlike Zechariah's question of unbelief, Mary simply wanted to know how this amazing thing would happen.

Here again is the upside-downness of the kingdom of God. Mary was probably thirteen or fourteen years old, physically small, voiceless as a girl in her culture, powerless to change her status in life. The God of the universe who made billions of stars and called them out by name chose to house himself in the fragile confines of a teenage girl's delicate womb. Oh, the humility, the mind-boggling plans of the Lord. He will not act according to our expectations or be restricted by our imaginations. His kingdom cannot be stopped. And far from forgetting his people, he would invade the quiet waiting of Israel in a flash of power and light next to the incense table in the temple. The silence had been broken. The Messiah of God's upside-down kingdom was coming.

Reflection Questions

4. What does God's use of Luke, and of all of who Luke is as a person, to tell this story communicate about how God intends to use us?

5. Reflect on the the thought that "there were no visions, no prophets, no word from Yahweh for over four hundred years," only rituals and routines to maintain a connection to the Lord. How must those four hundred years have felt? How does it make you view the spiritual habits we use on a regular basis in a different light?

6. Zechariah, the childless priest, bore the name that spoke the final truth over his personal story and the story of God's people, "the Lord has remembered." But in the years leading up to this moment, how do you think Zechariah viewed his story? Where are you currently in your view of your own personal story?

7. The angel had two different responses to the question that both Zechariah and Mary asked him. Speculate as to why that could be.

8. Mary was greeted with the phrase "O favored one," which in the Greek communicates that this is something that has been freely given, not earned. How does this affect your view of Mary? How do you see this phrase "O favored one" set upon you as well?

9. What does God using a doubting, childless priest and an unmarried teenager at this pivotal point in the history of his people tell us about who he is? What does it begin to reveal to us about the upside-down kingdom?

Focus verse: *"For nothing will be impossible with God." And Mary said, "Behold, I am the servant of the Lord; let it be to me according to your word." And the angel departed from her.*
Luke 1:37–38

Reflections, curiosities, frustrations:

Study 3

Songs and Prophecy Fulfilled

Read Luke 1:39-80

Observation Questions

1. Describe the interaction between Elizabeth and her cousin Mary in verses 39–45.

2. What specific actions of God does Mary reference in her song of praise (verses 46–55)?

3. What specific actions of God does Zechariah reference in his prophecy (verses 67–79)?

Verses 39–45. She went with haste. Wouldn't you? This teenager had to have been overwhelmed by her own news and curious about that of her elderly aunt. But hasty leaving would have turned into a four-day journey, full of time to ponder the way God was weaving together her story. We know Mary was given to contemplation, as the Gospel writers mention her tendency to "ponder all of these things in her heart." She had time, as she walked, to think about what the angel had said in terms of what she already knew about God. She would have known the stories of the Israelites, the story of Hannah, the hope of a Messiah to come. Imagine her putting the dots together and trying to wrap her head around the last few days.

By the movement of the Holy Spirit who apparently already resided within him, baby John heard and responded to Mary's voice. Does this sound too outlandish? Remember who is writing the story—the God who just created a baby in a virgin's womb. As Elizabeth's baby leapt for joy in her womb, she understood, seemingly in that moment, the grand story of which she was a part. It was really happening. The upside-down kingdom had come to her little town. And the king of the upside-down kingdom, tucked in underneath the heart of a teenage girl, had just entered her house.

Verses 46–56. Elizabeth's acknowledgment of the "Lord" was not lost on Mary. It seems that all of the pondering, the wonder of what was happening, the hopeful, "could it be?" thoughts that she must have had on the way to Elizabeth's house were confirmed. Her excitement and joy could no longer be contained, and they burst out of her in a song that is remarkably similar to Hannah's song in 1 Samuel 1, which she would have known since childhood. This is the Magnificat, sung by choirs for ages, named for the first word in the Latin version of the song, which literally means "enlarge." Mary could not help but worship as she acknowledged the privilege she had been given as mother of the Messiah. It was overwhelming. It was wonderful. And it was revolutionary.

Leon Morris describes this section of Mary's song as a "complete reversal of human values." First, the proud are brought down: "He has scattered the proud in the thoughts of their hearts" (verse 51). This is the death of pride. For where is there space for pride when a savior is so needed that he invades our broken world? Second, the mighty are brought down: "He has brought down the mighty from their thrones and exalted those of humble estate" (verse 52). The upside-down kingdom flips everything on its head. The humble take the place of power. What the world labels as important and influential will no longer be the standard. Third, the rich are brought down: "He has filled the hungry with good things, and the rich he has sent away empty" (verse 53). It was understood in Mary's day that the poor would always be hungry and the rich would always be full. The Messiah would reverse this, as in his kingdom the acquisition of goods was for the blessing of all. As Morris writes, "It is not the proud or the mighty or the rich who have the last word. Indeed, through his Messiah, God is about to overthrow all these. ... Mary sings of a God who is not bound by what people do. He turns human attitudes and orders of society upside down."

Verses 57–66. The day of a boy's circumcision was like our present-day infant baptism. Friends and relatives would have been invited to join the ceremony, which represented the child's inclusion into the covenant. It signified the fact that all of God's promises were now applicable to this one, too. It was also the day when the baby received his name from the parents. Apparently, the neighbors and relatives were already calling Elizabeth's child Zechariah. And why wouldn't they? This was the custom of the day. Although Elizabeth's pregnancy and Zechariah's vision in the temple were obviously unusual, the people of this little part of

Judea had no idea, yet, of the significance of John's birth. This was a break with tradition, a statement of God breaking in and calling John to something different. And those around this little family began to ponder, with Mary, what all of these things might mean.

Verses 67–80. Notice that Zechariah's first words after months of silence were words of praise. Filled with the Holy Spirit, he sang first about God keeping his promises to his people and then about his little son's calling to pave the way for the Messiah.

First, God was coming to his people. Here, a "horn of salvation," is a reference to the strength held in the horns of animals in the Near East. A strong salvation was in the works, giving hope of God's mercy. Remember that there had been silence for four hundred years. Finally, promises made centuries ago to Abraham would be remembered.

Second, Zechariah sang of his little boy's role. Malachi 4:5-6 reads, "Behold, I will send you Elijah the prophet before the great and awesome day of the LORD comes. And he will turn the hearts of fathers to their children and the hearts of children to their fathers, lest I come and strike the land with a decree of utter destruction." Most devout Jews believed that someone would come prior to the Messiah, an Elijah figure to prepare the way. Zechariah recognized John as this figure. God was answering both Zechariah's prayer for a child and his prayer for the deliverance of Israel. His song, as Mary's, spoke prophetically of things that were to come as if they had already happened. His song is one of overwhelming, relieved joy.

This is the overwhelming power, sovereignty, tenderness, and attention of our God. He is always working—both in our individual stories and in the bigger story of deliverance for his people. Just when we think there is nothing to be done, no way that he has heard all of our desperate pleas for some sort of redemption, he breaks through our expectations. He uses us in our frail and broken state for his own glory and purposes. What can our response be but that of Mary and Zechariah? We praise him. We tell the story of what he has done. We marvel at the way our God orders history so that the upside-down kingdom might come in its fullness.

Reflection Questions

4. As Mary traveled to Elizabeth's, in the quietness of her walk on the road, her mind must have been flooded with a million thoughts. What do you think she was thinking about? Why do you think she was eager to be with Elizabeth?

5. When Mary arrived at Elizabeth's house, she was greeted by her cousin speaking words from the Holy Spirit and John leaping in his mother's womb. Mary broke forth in song as centuries of prophecy came to life in this countryside house, carried in heart and body by two women. What's your response as you reflect on God ushering in his kingdom through two women?

6. Mary's response to all of this was to worship, or enlarge the story of God pursuing his children. What is one line from her song that really resonates with your heart? Why?

7. This gospel ended four hundred years of silence, a time in Israel's history when they felt so oppressed and forgotten. Based on Zechariah's prophecy, what do you think are some things God's people were longing for?

8. God answered both the individual prayers of Zechariah for a son and the collective prayers of him and Israel for a Messiah together in one story. What are some things that this shows us about the character of our God?

Focus verse: *Blessed be the Lord God of Israel, for he has visited and redeemed his people and raised up a horn of salvation for us in the house of his servant David.*
Luke 1:68-69

Reflections, curiosities, frustrations:

Study 4

Angels, Shepherds, and Temple Visits

Read Luke 2:1–52

Observation Questions

1. Why were Mary and Joseph in Bethlehem? Who were their first visitors after Jesus was born?

2. List the details of what happened the day Jesus was circumcised at the temple (who was there, what they each did, etc.).

3. List the details of what happened when Jesus was twelve years old and stayed behind in Jerusalem (who was there, what they each did, etc.).

Verses 1–7. The kingdom of man versus the kingdom of God. Oh, the contrast. Luke lays these out side by side. First, the kingdom of man: Augustus was taking a census either to figure out how many men he had for military campaigns or how many taxes he could collect. He was both appraising and displaying his power. Augustus, who had been adopted by Julius Caesar, declared his dead father to be divine and therefore declared himself to be a "son of god." He changed the Roman republic into an empire and asserted himself as "the savior of the world."

And the kingdom of God? The true Son of God was lying in a feeding trough. He was the child of a poor couple, and they had no one but Mary to wrap the baby in the traditional cloths, a job usually done by a midwife. He may have been born in a cave, the bottom floor of a house, or an open courtyard. As Leon Morris writes, "We do not know. We know only that everything points to poverty, obscurity, and even rejection." Jesus was not only physically poor but also poor in reputation at this point. Mary would not have legally needed to go with Joseph for the census, but it is quite probable that leaving Mary in Nazareth would have caused her to suffer the gossip and disdain of the entire village as she endured the last few months of her "illegitimate" pregnancy.

These two kingdoms could not have been more different. Augustus was building and displaying power for his own good.

God was entering into the brokenness of the world for our good. We must be warned: When we enter this upside-down kingdom, we join ourselves to the one who entered our world in every sort of poverty.

Verses 8-20. Most royal births are announced to the elite with a myriad of lavish ceremonies. This baby came with a holy army who sang to the outcasts. Shepherds were dirty, poor, and always ceremonially unclean because of their work. These shepherds, these unwanted people, were the recipients of the best news ever: The war between God and men was over; God was going to make peace—real peace.

Verses 21-40. Leviticus 12 tells us that when a woman had a baby, she was to bring a lamb as a burnt offering and a pigeon or turtle dove for a sin offering to make atonement for herself. However, if she could not afford a lamb, she could bring another pigeon or turtle dove instead. This, the offering Mary and Joseph brought, was called the "Offering of the Poor." So let's just put this into perspective. The one who authored history, marked the boundaries of the sea, and owned the cattle on a thousand hills was born into a family that couldn't afford a lamb. He was poor. And although his parents were clearly a devout part of the faithful remnant of Israel, they also probably struggled to put food on the table consistently.

What kind of a king starts out already behind, poor, at the bottom? Not the kind of king Israel expected. Jesus, from the very beginning of his humanity, dealt with the problem of suffering by entering into it. There was no escaping the cost of the peace he would bring. Mary would endure her own suffering because of Jesus's kingdom, as Simeon announced, but she would also see the glory that Anna proclaimed in the temple. It seems that those closest to Jesus and his kingdom will be those who know the most profound suffering, but also the most profound joy.

Verses 41–52. Were Joseph and Mary incredibly irresponsible parents? How did they forget their child? Travel caravans of Jesus's day would have been made up of many families travelling together and would have been divided between the men, who walked faster, and the women and children, who traveled much more slowly. The women would have left earlier in the day and the men later, meeting up to camp together at night. Since Jesus was just on the cusp of manhood, each parent could have easily assumed he was with the other group.

Every adult male who lived within fifteen miles of Jerusalem was required by Jewish law to attend the Passover. At twelve, Jesus was considered a man. Imagine him walking around the temple, watching the priests, smelling the smoke from the lambs burning on the altar. He would have understood the purpose of the blood and the ritual, the need for cleansing and forgiveness. He, more than any twelve-year-old, knew how great the distance was between the Jews and the God they worshipped. Somehow, his self-awareness had grown to the point that when his parents returned to find him, Jesus's first words included referring to God as Father, instead of his earthly father, Joseph.

The temple was the regular place where teachers would have gathered to discuss the Scriptures. While Mary was rushed and panicked, Jesus was calm. He had found his place in his "Father's house" with an understanding of the Scriptures and God that amazed the theological experts of his day. His parents, the people who knew him best, completely misunderstood him in this moment. Jesus had connected the dots. He knew who he was, and it was not what his parents expected.

Isn't this true for us? We have experiences that cause us to believe we know Jesus, that we've figured him out. And then he surprises us. This is the upside-down kingdom of God, where the true king is born into poverty, his birth announcement is sent to the outcasts, his future is declared to be wrapped up with suffering, and his relationship with us is never what we expect.

Reflection Questions

4. Mary and Joseph's poverty resulted in Jesus's birth in impoverished conditions, with nothing but a feeding trough for a bed. What about Jesus coming under such conditions surprises you? What about it makes you uncomfortable?

5. The unclean, untrustworthy, unwanted shepherds were the first to be greeted by a host of angels to tell them that the Messiah had come. What do you think God is trying to communicate about the gospel through this scene? Have you found this to be true of the gospel?

6. Jesus started out his life on earth in a state of poverty and suffering, making him well acquainted with the hard parts of this life. In what ways can that affect the way you pray to him about your suffering and life?

7. At age twelve Jesus began to exercise his calling in different, more obvious ways, like staying back to learn from the scribes and teachers in the synagogue while his family went home. When have you made intentional choices resulting in kingdom-minded living?

8. Jesus surprised his parents when he chose not to leave Jerusalem when they did, showing them that who they thought he was, and how he should act, looked different than expected. When has your idea of who you thought Jesus was shifted or changed? Why?

Focus verse: *And he said to them, "Why were you looking for me? Did you not know that I must be in my Father's house?" And they did not understand the saying that he spoke to them.*
Luke 2:49-50

Reflections, curiosities, frustrations:

Study 5

Read Luke 3:1–38

Observation Questions

1. From verses 7–14, write the words and phrases John the Baptist said to the people.

2. From verses 21-22, write the specific details of Jesus's baptism.

3. Write the names that you recognize from the genealogy of Jesus (verses 23–38). List what you know about them.

Verses 1-9. Eighteen years had passed since Jesus had called the living God his Father while sitting at the temple in Jerusalem. Luke carefully brings us up to speed by placing his story in its political and religious context, finally narrowing to one man in one region. The word of God had come to John. Little is said about this last great prophet, but his message is clear: Get ready. Judgment is coming. You must repent.

All of John's words and work pointed to someone else. John was the courier, the hype man, the forerunner for Jesus. He quoted Isaiah 40:3-5, encouraging the people to ready themselves for the coming king. In ancient times, when kings wanted to visit a portion of their territory, they would send a courier ahead to those along the way, telling them to ready the course: fill in the holes, straighten the road, build bridges, cut down trees. They had to remove whatever was necessary to prepare a path so that the king could get to them. Jesus was a different kind of king, requiring a different kind of preparation, one of the heart.

John's harsh words were directed toward those Jews who thought that their spiritual pedigree was a free ticket into the kingdom. Although being biologically related to Abraham is a huge privilege, it isn't what finally determines entrance into God's kingdom. Everyone must enter as an individual, responding by faith to Jesus's call. Baptism in John's day was a ceremony used for unclean Gentiles converting to Judaism. It would have been offensive to the Jews to hear John preach of their need for such a rite, since they believed they were already "in."

What about us? Does the call to repentance offend you? Do you consider yourself too mature for such a basic movement in your life with the Lord? Do you close your ears or gloss over the call to repentance given by John, deciding it is only for those who have never aligned themselves with this king? Beware, dear one. In this kingdom, we never get beyond repentance. It is the starting place, the middle place, and the ending place of life with the king.

Verses 10-20. Obviously not all in the crowd were hard-hearted. Their genuine response brought John's practical advice for moral change. He did not instruct them to quit their jobs or destroy the system in which they worked, but to do their jobs in a conscientious and ethical way. Those who had enough were to share with those who did not. Tax collectors who made a living by taking extra money were only to take what they needed. Jewish soldiers working for Rome were to treat civilians fairly, not using extortion or bribes. These were huge behavioral changes in their culture. Real repentance isn't a feeling or mere words. It has teeth, action, and perceptible change. John was calling these men and women, and still calls us through his words, to an actual adjustment of conduct. As Sinclair Ferguson says, "Repentance throws into reverse gear the patterns of sin that have dominated you."

Notice John's singular focus on the coming one's glory and position. Crowds were coming to John to listen. His following was growing, as was his influence as a teacher and prophet. But John redirected any attention or popularity to the better teacher who was to come. Apparently teachers were paid not with money in ancient Palestine but with favors. According to a rabbinic saying, anything a slave would do for his master was a fair expectation of a disciple for his teacher, except for one task: untying a sandal thong.

Loosing dirty foot straps was too degrading even for a disciple. But the one that was coming would be like no teacher anyone had ever served. No task would be menial in his service. Not only would he baptize with the Spirit; he would judge between those who would be gathered in and those who would be burned.

Verses 21–22. Jesus heard about his cousin preaching and baptizing in the wilderness. Notice his approach. Just as he had chosen to join himself to sinners in his birth, so he chose to identify with sinners by being baptized. Jesus had no need for repentance or cleansing. But this is his way. He is always coming nearer to us.

In a moment of amazing intimacy displayed for all around, God affirmed his son and his ministry. God's words pointed to Jesus's future. "You are my beloved Son" is a part of Psalm 2:7, a description of the Messiah. But Jesus knew that the same Messiah would die for the sins of Israel. Even on this day, the public beginning of his ministry, Jesus knew where he was going. He was not being crowned as a privileged prince, destined for wealth and power. Jesus was beginning the road to the cross.

Verses 23–38. It is easy for us to forget that while Jesus was fully God, he was also fully human. The genealogy at the end of the chapter is further evidence of this. Though he clearly understood something of his identity in the temple at age twelve, Jesus returned with his parents to Nazareth, submitted to their authority, and waited. It is clear that Jesus's family was poor. He knew long hours and lean meals. Hebrews 5:8 tells us, "Although he was a son, he learned obedience through what he suffered." In this upside-down kingdom, the king himself entered into the tiresome, mundane tasks of everyday life. The servant of the Lord, the Messiah, labored among human tools and scraps of wood in order to provide for the least of these. And although he was without sin, he suffered, in all the ways we do, in the brokenness of the world he came to save.

Reflection Questions

4. John the Baptist had a unique role of being the courier and hype man for Jesus, to prepare the people's hearts for their encounter with the Lord. What in John's words or phrases from this text has prepared your heart in a new way for Jesus?

5. As we see in this passage, the call to repentance is a crucial part of every believer's life. How would you describe repentance and its role in your life?

6. At this point in history untying someone's sandal was considered beneath even the lowest in society. Yet Jesus comes and serves in humility. What does this teach us about his desire to be near us?

7. At Jesus's baptism we get to see this very tender, intimate proclamation of God toward his Son, connecting back to Scriptures the Jews would have known describing the suffering Messiah. What does this moment show us about God the Father toward Jesus his Son? How does that connect to us?

8. There are several years of life between Jesus at age twelve at the temple and his baptism as a grown man. The years were filled with day-to-day mundane tasks of work and family life. Not all of his days were lived in public ministry. How does this thought change your perspective on the different seasons in your life?

Focus verse: *And the Holy Spirit descended on him in bodily form, like a dove; and a voice came from heaven, "You are my beloved Son; with you I am well pleased."*
Luke 3:22

Reflections, curiosities, frustrations:

Study 6

Satan's Temptations and Jesus's Authority

Read Luke 4:1–44

Observation Questions

1. What are the three things with which the devil tried to tempt Jesus?

2. Describe what happened in the synagogue in Nazareth (who was there, what they did, etc.).

3. Verses 31–44 describe the beginning of Jesus's ministry. List some of the things he did.

Verses 1–13. Jesus went from a climactic spiritual high to a wretched, arduous low. Notice that the Spirit led him into the desert to be tempted. This is always the way for the leaders God chooses. He tests and readies them before he uses them. He did the same thing with his Son. In the midst of this wrestling, Satan showed up. He inserted himself, whether in some visible form or just in the mind of Jesus, and offered various possibilities for ministry. Satan is not stupid. He does not offer us things that will not be attractive. Instead, he follows, watches, and waits for an opportune time. Then he offers an alternative that will seem to help accomplish our goal or meet our legitimate need but will do so while leading us away from dependency on and obedience to God.

This is the life of a saint (which you are, dear one, if you are a believer). It is a life of testing, of wrestling, of being formed by the Spirit who led Jesus into the desert in the first place. Notice that the devil only left him until a better situation presented itself. Satan never stops lying, never stops attempting to convince us to take the way of ease and independence instead of struggle and dependence on God. All testing reveals our hearts. Jesus's heart was revealed to be pure, ready to accept the cross, and utterly dependent on his Father.

Verses 14–22. Jesus went on a preaching tour, and the crowds continued to grow. When he finally returned to his hometown, he attended the synagogue, where teaching and discussion about the Scriptures usually happened. There would not have been a regular priest or rabbi. Instead, all adult men were called upon to read a part of the law, read some from the prophets, and then make comments. Everyone who was in the synagogue that day knew Jesus, probably from the time he was a boy. Yet they had heard the reports and were probably hoping that he might that very day begin his conquest. They expected him to launch his plan for routing the Romans and bringing down a corrupt political system. They all believed that the Jews were God's chosen people and that Gentiles were simply, as rabbis wrote, "fuel for the fires of hell." They thought, as long as they had a Jewish heritage, they had only to wait for the Messiah to come and put everyone else in their place.

Everyone was listening expectantly as Jesus read from Isaiah 61. "The year of the Lord's favor" would have reminded them of the Year of Jubilee, which happened once every fifty years. In that year, according to Leviticus 25, all debts were forgiven and slaves set free. Jesus sat down, the posture of any man teaching in the synagogue, and then he said it: "Today this Scripture has been fulfilled in your hearing." Yes! Their hearts must have leapt. What we hoped for is true! Jesus was claiming to be the object of Isaiah's prophecy. The long awaited one had come. He would rescue the Jews and put others in the lower place. So they thought.

Verses 22-30. In that moment Jesus could have made a very different choice. He could have given the people exactly what they wanted—rescue from political oppression and some sort of favored, exclusive salvation for Jews. But Jesus had known this moment would come, and he had prepared himself to build a kingdom not only for the Jews but for all who would come to him. He knew, as he always knows, the hearts of those around him. He knew they wanted signs. He also knew he would anger them. And yet he boldly called them out. He confronted their prideful belief that God loved only them. Using the Scriptures they would have known, he pointed out God's pursuit of Gentiles even in the time of their ancestors. And it enraged them. They expected and understood some sort of grace for their own kind, but this was too much. Grace extended to the dirty, unceremoniously clean Gentiles pushed them over the edge.

Before we scowl at these people and judge them for their clueless closed-mindedness, we might examine ourselves for a moment. Do we do this? Do we consider certain categories of people outside the realm of Jesus's grace? What about the child abusers? The scandal-laden politicians? The fill-in-the-blank wretched people whom you cannot consider objects of salvation? What might Jesus say to you about these people?

Verses 31–37. Here, at the beginning of his ministry, we begin to catch glimpses of Jesus's astonishing authority. Two things happened in Galilee at the synagogue that reveal his jurisdiction over all things. First, his teaching. Rabbis at the time of Jesus did most of their teaching by quoting rabbis that had come before them, and some did this exclusively. Enter Jesus's teaching. He quoted no one except Old Testament writers. His was not a delegated authority. He simply spoke the truth about God. The people who listened to him had never heard anything like this. No wonder they were astonished.

Secondly, this authority extended to Jesus's interactions with demons. Apparently a holy war had been launched, and "the demons knew it." Their territory was being threatened. Notice how they spoke to Jesus. There was no doubt for the demon who Jesus was and that Jesus had the ability to destroy it. Demons and exorcism were a common occurrence at this point in history. However, unlike those usually exorcising demons, Jesus did not use magical words, strange ceremonies, or the conjuring of some greater power. He simply told the demon to shut up and come out. And it did. Again, his was not some secondary authority. As we learn later in the Gospels, all authority had already been given to this king. And so he only needed to speak to make things happen. Jesus was fulfilling the prophecy Isaiah had made about him. He was proclaiming good news to the poor and setting the captives free.

Verses 38-44. Once again we see Jesus's unmatched authority. He had no need for medicines or incantations. He simply spoke to the sickness, and it left. This was a Sabbath day, meaning that no work could be done by the Jews, including the work of carrying the sick. But when the sun set, the sick and demon possessed quickly found Jesus. See his tenderness, which Luke points out, how he touched each individual person as he healed them. We know from later stories in Luke that Jesus did not need to have physical contact with someone to heal him. Consider the dignity he bestowed on each person who desperately approached him for healing. He, God incarnate, laid his hands on them.

Why did Jesus keep rebuking the demons? They clearly knew the truth about him, in contrast to the crowds who would take much longer to understand his identity. Why not let them proclaim his messiahship? Because this was not an ordinary kingdom, where the king grasps for power from any and all parties. The kingdom of God, which Luke first records Jesus naming in verse 43, had a different kind of Messiah than what was expected by the Jews. It was a politically tense time in Palestine, and announcement of a Messiah could have sparked nationalistic messianic movements leading to great upheavals and physical danger. Jesus had the long game in mind. With his authority, over and over in word and deed, he would demonstrate for them what God's kingdom and God's rule looked like. This king was one who had entered the suffering of the world and served his subjects with humility. The upside-down kingdom was on display among the sick and the demon possessed, as the servant of God preached his way through the synagogues of Judea.

Reflection Questions

4. Satan's interaction with Jesus details for us how he does this in our life as well. Where in your life do you struggle to not believe the lies of Satan and to not give into his temptations?

5. The Jews were so angry at Jesus for teaching the inclusion of the Gentiles that they tried to throw him off a cliff. What person or people group do you get angry at when you think they could be forgiven and receive the grace found in the gospel?

6. One way Jesus starts his ministry is by going to the synagogue and reading the Scriptures. What does this teach us about the importance of us knowing the full counsel of God?

7. Jesus has complete power and authority even over the demons. What about that is comforting to you? What about that is scary or unsettling?

8. Jesus healed those who came to him, laying his hands on every one of them, even though touch was not required for healing them. What does this say about Jesus's compassion for our pain and suffering? When, if ever, have you experienced this from him?

Focus verse: *And they were all amazed and said to one another, "What is this word? For with authority and power he commands the unclean spirits, and they come out!"*
Luke 4:36

Reflections, curiosities, frustrations:

Study 7

The New Disciples and Unexpected Healings

Read Luke 5:1–39

Observation Questions

1. Describe what happened when Jesus called the first five of his twelve disciples.

2. What did Jesus say to the leper and the paralytic when he healed them? What were the witnesses' reactions?

3. What were the Pharisees' reactions when Jesus called Levi the tax collector and ate with his friends?

At His Feet

Verses 1-11. The "Hound of Heaven," as Jesus has been called, was after a fisherman named Simon. Simon had heard Jesus's teaching and had seen his power. Remember that Jesus had been in Simon's house and healed his mother-in-law. Simon had seen him heal the sick and free people from demon possession after the sun had set on that Sabbath day. He had surely heard him preach in the synagogue. These two men had some sort of relationship. But Jesus was much more sure about Simon than Simon was about Jesus.

It was Simon's boat that Jesus borrowed one day to speak to the crowds that were now inevitable wherever he went. Simon surely listened as he spoke to the people that morning near the water. After speaking, Jesus narrowed his focus to Simon. "Put out into the deep and let down your nets for a catch," he commanded. Simon was no amateur fisherman. This was his area of expertise, and he believed nothing would come of trying again at this point. But he had also seen enough of Jesus to know that he should listen. And so he obeyed.

The catch of fish that resulted from listening to Jesus was the biggest any of the professional fishermen in those boats had ever seen. They could have cashed in, celebrated, and called it a good day at work. But what they had just learned about the true king who had demonstrated his dominion over all things had captivated their hearts. Simon could no longer hold in a response. It's as if he had watched, quietly, all of the miracles, the words, the healings, and they were too much for him. "Depart from me, for I am a sinful man, O Lord," he said. If we see ourselves clearly at all when we see the blinding majesty and power of Jesus, this will be our response. We have no right to be near such kindness, perfection, and purity. The holiness of God and the sinfulness of humans cannot coexist. And yet, Jesus, already knowing all of the terrible parts of Simon, pursued him, in a very particular and personal way, calling him as a disciple.

This is how he calls us. He keeps showing up, speaking to us through other people or his Word. He woos us by his power, his character, his love. And then in an individual way, he calls us to be his disciple. Is he doing this for you, even now?

Verses 12-26. Luke, the doctor, always careful to point out the physical condition and healing of people, is no less thorough in his description of Jesus's spiritual, emotional, and relational healing. First, the leper. It would be a fair to assume this man had not been touched in years. In order to prevent accidental spread of the disease, any infected person would have to yell out "Unclean, unclean!" as he walked anywhere near healthy people. People with leprosy would have been estranged from family, unable to earn a living, sometimes disfigured, and definitely isolated.   As Leon Morris points out, "The psychological effects of all this seem to have been as serious as the physical." Notice Jesus's touch and reassurance: "I will; be clean." But Jesus didn't stop there. Jesus's command for the man to obey Moses would have ensured that the priest would have examined him, declared him clean, and restored him to community. Jesus's healing does not stop at the physical. His kingdom will ultimately bring total emotional, relational, psychological, and spiritual restoration.

Second, the paralytic. Jesus knew that the man's greatest need, even above his need to move his own body, was his need of forgiveness, of spiritual restoration.   So he granted it. This infuriated the Pharisees, who were the unofficial religious leaders of the day. The Pharisees, whose name meant "separated ones," built laws around the laws given by God, just to be sure no one broke them. But they had entirely missed the intent of the law, which was meant to point them to Jesus himself.

Verses 27-32. Levi is called by the name Matthew in other Gospels. He was probably the wealthiest of the disciples, having been a tax collector. Tax collectors were hated, unclean, untrusted people. "As a class they were regarded as dishonest," Leon Morris explains. Levi invites his new Lord to spend time with his friends, who also would have been tax collectors. In Jesus's day, eating with someone signified a kind of love for a person that the Pharisees and scribes were unwilling to extend to these outcasts who didn't come close to keeping the law. The religious leaders worried that sinners would make them defiled and unclean. Jesus, however, came to make these unclean sinners beautifully holy.

Verses 33–39. Again, the Pharisees missed the point in their question to Jesus about fasting. Though fasting was only prescribed once per year by the law, the Pharisees made it their practice to fast twice per week. As one commentator notes, "Fasting reflects a condition of dissatisfaction, if not of grief." They were living weekly as if it was a time to mourn for Israel, as if the kingdom had not yet come. But the kingdom had come. The king was standing right in front of them. Jesus compares his presence to a wedding, something to be celebrated. A wedding is a celebratory feast, not a place of mourning. He explains his kingdom to them as a new garment and as new wine. The new simply cannot be fitted onto or poured into the old.

The upside-down kingdom was not like anything the people in Galilee had seen before. Its king did not sit on a throne and summon followers from afar, demanding their fitness before approaching him. He got into the old, stinky boat of a fisherman and showed his power through fish. He approached a completely isolated, untouchable man and showed his love through touch. He announced forgiveness to a man who needed his friends to even get to Jesus. He chose as one of his closest allies a societal outcast. This is the upside-down kingdom, where the king leaves his throne and enters any and every realm necessary to call us to himself.

Reflection Questions

4. After a frustrating night of fishing without a catch, Simon and his companions must have been discouraged. Jesus entered in and filled their nets to overflowing. Describe a time when God completely changed the outcome of a circumstance in your favor.

5. Simon, after watching Jesus teach, heal, and get him his biggest catch of his lifetime, responded with, "Depart from me, for I am a sinful man, O Lord." Why do you think he responded this way? Have you ever felt this way when you have encountered Jesus?

6. Jesus healed both the leper and the paralytic in holistic ways, not just physically. For the leper, he restored him to community; for the paralytic, he forgave his sins. Where in your life have you seen the gospel of Jesus bring holistic healing?

7. The Pharisees, or "separated ones," were looking for the Messiah. Their rules kept them from seeing it was Jesus. How are you currently like them?

8. Which of these moments in the upside-down kingdom does your heart most need to engage with right now: calling of the fishermen, healing the untouchable, forgiving the paralytic, or associating with outcasts? Why?

Focus verse: *After this he went out and saw a tax collector named Levi, sitting at the tax booth. And he said to him, "Follow me." And leaving everything, he rose and followed him.*
Luke 5:27-28

Reflections, curiosities, frustrations:

Study 8

Upside-Down Blessing

Read Luke 6:1-26

Observation Questions

1. What are the two things Jesus did on the Sabbath? Who disagreed with him for this? Why?

2. What did Jesus do before he called the disciples? List the disciples' names.

3. What four things did Jesus count as blessings? What four things did he name as woes?

Verses 1–11. The ceremonial law was a means to an end, a signpost for something greater, a shadow of what was to come. But the Pharisees had made obeying the ceremonial law an end in itself. As they continued to try to trap Jesus in an old system, he showed them not only that they misunderstood its purpose but that he had authority over the law. First, Jesus's followers harvested on the Sabbath. While walking through the grain fields, the disciples picked some grains, rubbed them between their fingers, and ate. The Pharisees, who were obviously spying on them, thought they'd caught Jesus's disciples. Always seeking to indict Jesus for breaking the law, they interpreted the picking as harvesting, the rubbing as threshing, the throwing away of the chaff as winnowing, and the eating as somehow preparing food—all things forbidden on the Sabbath. But Jesus referred them to the story of David and his companions eating the bread of the presence in the tabernacle (1 Samuel 21:6). Only the priests were supposed to eat this bread, which signified the presence of God. But, as one commentator points out, "Ceremonial rites (being only means to an end) must give way to a higher moral law." Human need trumped ritual. And just as David, when he ate the temple bread, was the anointed king but not yet recognized by all of Israel, so Jesus was the anointed king but not yet recognized by the new Israel he would call.

Second, Jesus healed on the Sabbath. While the Pharisees allowed healing when someone was in danger of dying, healing a man with a shriveled hand who obviously was not in any immediate danger was strictly forbidden. Notice the difference between Jesus and the religious establishment. The Pharisees thought they were protecting and following every law. Jesus was also determined to follow the law: "For truly, I say to you, until heaven and earth pass away, not an iota, not a dot, will pass from the Law until all is accomplished" (Matt. 5:18). However, it is clear that Jesus and the Pharisees had different understandings of both the requirements and the purpose of God's law.

Though the man was not in danger of death, he was suffering, and probably had been for many years. Certainly the Pharisees thought Jesus had walked right into their trap unknowingly. But Jesus knew their thoughts. And so while they thought they were setting him up, he set them up with a question. He left no middle ground but offered only the choice to do good or evil. All their additions, explanations, and expansions of the law had not brought clarity. Instead, quite the opposite had happened. They had tortured God's holy law of love into something so unrecognizable that it blinded them from fulfilling the chief purpose of the law. What God intended for good by instituting the Sabbath, they had twisted and corrupted into evil. In this question, then, Jesus exposed that their unwillingness to heal that had entirely turned around God's purposes for the Sabbath. God gave the Sabbath to provide life-giving rest to the weary (Ex. 20:10), but they had turned it into an oppressive weapon. Thus, the Pharisees missed the point of the Sabbath, and they were furious at Jesus for daring to defy their legalistic decrees. The Son of Man, as Jesus loved to call himself, did not come to shame, trap, or catch you doing wrong like the Pharisees. He came to save. He came to have mercy. And more than that, he came to lead his people into the Sabbath rest that remains for the people of God (Heb. 4:9). He came, as he read from Isaiah in Luke 4:18, to proclaim good news to the poor, freedom for the prisoners, sight for the blind, and freedom for the oppressed and to proclaim the year of the Lord's favor. His presence was good news; his kingdom brought and still brings wholeness and restoration, both physical and spiritual.

Verses 12–16. Opposition was growing. Jesus must have known that at some point the religious establishment would find a way to kill him. He had come with unbelievably good news, but time was short. How would he get the message of the kingdom out to the world before he was silenced? In a characteristic move, Jesus prayed, this time all night. As he had been alone in the desert with God before the start of his ministry, listening and pondering, so he was alone with God again. And like Moses came down from the mountain after spending time with God and spoke to the twelve tribes of Israel, Jesus came back to his disciples and chose twelve men, the foundation on which he would build his church.

Who were these spiritual giants called to be the first of a church that must endure until the Second Coming? Here again is the astonishing difference of the upside-down kingdom. Jesus chose such ordinary, unexpected men: fishermen, a tax collector, a zealot who had probably encouraged revolutionary opposition to Rome. Jesus, the one who knew the hearts of men, chose one who would betray him. Who builds a leadership team like this? Only one whose kingdom was nothing like the world had ever seen.

Verses 17–26. Jesus had reached the point in his ministry where it was hard to be alone. Everywhere he went, crowds followed. They couldn't get enough of him. Not only did he speak with authority; he healed all kinds of diseases and cast out demons with power. It is no wonder that large crowds of people literally traveled for days to listen to, see, and touch him. As Jesus spoke, taught, and healed, he had begun to show the crowds and especially the disciples a new kind of kingdom, a new way of community. As we read his words, it is easy for us to gloss over them if we've read them many times before. So let's read them in a new context.

Imagine you're going on a trip to a new country with a small group of friends. Your guide has lived in the country of your destination before and therefore speaks the language and understands the customs. While you make travel plans, your guide explains to you what you need to know about the people you'll be visiting. To be most helpful, he gives you a list of values. What does the culture prize? What is most important to them? Is it family? Loyalty? Freedom? How do they react to bad news? Do they grieve? Stuff it? Are they a celebratory culture? As you listen to your leader, you get a sense of the people, how they handle the joy and losses of life and what motivates them.

This is what Jesus is doing in this passage. He is describing a new community by giving the disciples a list of kingdom values. And to describe the new community even more clearly, he gives them another list for comparison—that of their current world. First, the values of the kingdom: powerlessness, neediness, grief, and exclusion. The word "poor" in verse 20 could be understood as powerless or poor in spirit. The word "hungry" in verse 21 is used in contrast to being full or comfortable, having your sensory needs met. To "weep" here in verse 21 refers to grieving in general at the brokenness and sadness of the world.

"Blessed" here means "deeply satisfied." We could read this passage this way: In my kingdom, there is deep satisfaction when you are powerless. Only then can you know the wealth and power of the coming kingdom. There is deep blessing when you are needy. Then I can satisfy your need with myself. You are privileged when you grieve now about the brokenness and sin in the world. Why? Because you will laugh with joy later when I set it right. You are favored if you are excluded now because of your connection to me, because that exclusion will lead to great reward later. The conditions of neediness and dependency on God are the things that we prize in the kingdom of God. Why? Because that deep contentment that you know when you are connected to Jesus is completely unaffected by circumstances. In fact, when you are weak, needy, grieving, or excluded, the power and delight you have in Jesus somehow grows stronger.

Now for the contrast. What are the values of the world, both for us and the disciples? Power, comfort, success, and recognition. These are spelled out in verses 24-26. "Woe to you" does not convey the sadness and pity these words represent. It would be better to translate them, "how terrible" or "how awful."

"'Woe to you' is an expression of regret and compassion, not a threat," explains Leon Morris. We might read these verses in this way: How terrible for the woman who is rich only with money. She has all she will ever receive. How sad for the woman who is physically satisfied but feels no spiritual hunger. She will be hungry later. How awful to be that man who gloats about his success now, never grieving. He will grieve later. How sad to be the man with so many fans, who never says anything hard or truthful. He's like the smooth talkers before him. It's not that power, comfort, success, and recognition are bad things or things to be avoided in and of themselves. There are many examples of godly men and women in the Bible who have all of these things. It is only that we must be suspect of them, and free from their control. These things can encourage self-reliance and the belief that we are not needy like the poor or the grieving.

How bizarre are these statements of Jesus? He completely turns the values of the world upside down. Leon Morris writes, "Together with the ... woes, these beatitudes make a mockery of the world's values. They exalt what the world despises and reject what the world admires." In fact, Jesus knew a kind of happiness that was deeper and more resistant to suffering than anything the world could offer. As we seek to live out the community of Jesus's upside-down kingdom, we may often feel like we are in constant trouble as our values rub up against what is prized by the world. But remember Jesus's words about what is true for disciples in his kingdom: yours is the kingdom of God, you will be satisfied, you will laugh, and your reward is great in heaven. May his words lead to our fearlessness and absurd happiness.

Reflection Questions

4. Jesus fulfilled the law in the deepest way by showing mercy and healing on the Sabbath. Why do you think this made the Pharisees angry? Can you relate to their reaction?

5. In verse 9, Jesus uses a question to expose and connect to the Pharisees' hearts. How often do you ask questions of yourself or others? How could you grow in this area?

6. Before Jesus, fully God and fully man, called his disciples, he spent the whole night in prayer. What does this teach us about the importance of prayer for us?

7. Which "blessed are you" or "deeply satisfied are you" from the list in the text have you experienced the most in your relationship with the Lord? When?

8. Which "woe to you" or "how awful for you" from the list in the text have you experienced the most in your life or seen in the lives around you? When?

Focus verse: *And he lifted up his eyes on his disciples, and said: "Blessed are you who are poor, for yours is the kingdom of God."*
Luke 6:20

Reflections, curiosities, frustrations:

Study 9

Enemies, Judging Others, and Fruitlessness

Read Luke 6:27-49

Observation Questions

1. List the things Jesus said to do for others in verses 27-36.

2. In verses 37-42, how did Jesus say we should relate to our brothers and sisters?

3. In verses 46-49, how did Jesus describe the man who hears his words and does them?

Verses 27–36. The Greeks recognized four kinds of love: *eros* (passionate, between lovers), *storge* (familial, between sisters), *philia* (teamlike, like a brotherhood of common interests as in soldiers in a war or players on a team), and *agape* (parental, mature, sacrificial). Unlike the other types of love, *agape* is in no way related to the attractiveness of the object. It does not occur because of common interests or possible payback. Its aim is the absolute good of the object. This is the kind of love Jesus tells us to lavish on our enemies.

Jesus is painting a picture, describing a principle. He is not calling us to passivity in the face of abuse, or voluntary poverty. Leon Morris writes, "Once again it is the spirit of the saying that is important. If Christians took this one absolutely literally there would soon be a class of saintly paupers, owning nothing, and another of prosperous idlers and thieves. It is not this that Jesus is seeking, but a readiness among his followers to give and give and give. The Christian should never refrain from giving out of a love for his possessions. Love must be ready to be deprived of everything if need be. But it is love that must decide whether we give or withhold, not a regard for our possessions." *Agape* is love that makes decisions based on the good of its object. It is not blind to the faults and undeserving nature of its object, but clear-eyed. It is active and purposeful, strong and God-motivated. It is something of the will. Loving in this way is actively choosing, from a place of power, to operate out of a law of love rather than the law of control. It is seeking the good of others, even when they don't deserve it, and even when they don't seek yours. It is a kind of death to self. It is sacrificial. It is not only not retaliating but trying to figure out what is something I can do for this person that would bring her good?

This is a hard command. If it doesn't feel hard, consider who comes to mind when you think about someone who has hurt you, wished you harm, been cruel, or actively fought against what you want or believe. Then read the above paragraph again. Loving our enemies is an act of the will. Yet somehow it cannot just be cold duty, a legalistic task that is then checked off our list. This is an extremely high calling, a call to be like God. If this does not give us pause, we have overestimated ourselves. When we try to do this we will absolutely come up against our limitations and feelings of angst, maybe even disgust. We will find ourselves begging God to change us to be more like him, asking for the anger and resentment we feel toward our enemies to be taken from us. When we truly try to love our enemies, we will find that we can only do so if we are overwhelmed by God's tender and powerful love for us, who were once his enemies.

Are you having trouble naming your enemy? Maybe it's the neighbor who has the opposite political affiliation, puts offensive signs in his yard, and advocates for policy that you abhor. Maybe it's the boss who shows favoritism and never gives you credit. What would it look like to work for the good of the coworker who is never kind? How could you bless the relative who belittles you for your faith at every family gathering? Again, this is a hard word from our Lord. Jesus is telling us that his followers cannot be selective in their love. We don't love with *agape* to gain access to God, or even to be rewarded by him, though he says we will be. We do so because God does so. We do so because he is our dad, and kids act like their dad. We do so because "while we were enemies we were reconciled to God by the death of his Son" (Romans 5:10). We show *agape* to those who don't deserve it because we take Jesus at his word, and this is his command.

Verses 37–42. It may seem that Jesus is mixing topics when, in the middle of talking about judgment and mercy, he suddenly mentions giving. While these verses about giving have perpetually been taken out of context and used to encourage the giving of money, Jesus is actually talking about giving mercy. When we judge, we are like the Pharisees, condemning others based on a standard we cannot keep. Jesus tells us in these three short paragraphs that instead of following in the footsteps of the Pharisees and condemning others, we should deal with our own sin and give mercy to others. For us, there is no room to judge. There is only Jesus's call to repentance.

In verse 37, Jesus tells us not to judge others. The "lap" or "bosom" mentioned in verse 38 comes from a part of the clothing worn in Jesus's time. One commentator explains: "Almost all ancient nations wore long, wide, and loose garments; and when about to carry anything which their hands could not contain, they used a fold of their robe in nearly the same way as women here use their aprons." Jesus was saying that when you generously give mercy to people when they sin against you, God will generously give mercy to you when you sin against him. In fact, his mercy to you will overflow like grain overflowing from your pockets during harvest time.

In verses 39–40, Jesus is talking about choosing whom we follow. He has been instructing his disciples to give mercy and refrain from judgment. This is the exact opposite of what the Pharisees and teachers of the law spent their time doing. A little bit of cultural context is helpful here. In the region of Palestine, water was and still is a precious commodity. People would dig for water and, finding none, would often abandon the holes as unmarked pits. The blind folks of the day, which were many, easily fell into these pits, often causing catastrophic injury. Jesus is warning those listening that the religious leaders of the day were spiritually blind, and that if people followed them, they, too, would eventually be blind like their leaders, leading to their destruction.

In verses 41–42, we get to see a little bit of Jesus's humor, which should not be overlooked. He is creating a caricature of the Pharisees as they bumble around with huge logs in their eyes. The word for "log" here refers to the main beam of a house, a massive piece of wood. All the while they were attempting to remove a small chip from someone else's eye. They couldn't have gotten close enough to anyone else to even see another's eye. This is foolishness! The Pharisees couldn't help anyone because they couldn't see their own sin.

Verses 43–49. Jesus had more words for those listening to him who were no doubt trying to decide whom to follow as their authoritative religious leader. The Pharisees and teachers of the law had gone to extreme measures to be sure that their outward appearances aligned with their idea of righteousness—the keeping of the law. But this did nothing for their hearts. They could check off all of the requirements they set for themselves and still be full of hatred, resentment, lust, and so on. This is Jesus's point with his words about the tree. The only real way to see the health of the tree is to look at its fruit. If the fruit is rotten, so is the tree. The teaching that came out of the Pharisees was not life giving but rotten.

In the last short parable in this section (verses 46–49), Jesus pushes the choice of whom to follow to the forefront. He leaves no gray area for the people's response to him and his teaching. The choices are clear: Either hear my words and put them into practice, leading to salvation, or ignore my words, leading to destruction. Jesus frequently narrowed our spiritual choices down to just two: life or death, salvation or destruction, for him or against him. These words easily offend our modern ears. But make no mistake, dear ones. The warnings of this shepherd king are those of love. He was calling disciples then, as he is now, to the upside-down kingdom. In his kingdom, enemies are loved not because they deserve it but because the king chose to love them. Mercy is given lavishly, because it has been given lavishly by God. Instead of criticizing our brothers and sisters, we look first at our own sin. And salvation from our total destruction comes from the strong foundation of the rock himself.

Reflection Questions

4. Who is the enemy that came to mind when reading this passage and commentary? What is the hardest part about applying *agape* love to that situation?

5. Jesus's call of loving your enemies has a lot to do with loving others more than loving our possessions. When is this hard for you?

6. Jesus's call in verses 37-42 is to overflow your brothers and sisters with mercy instead of judgement, resulting in God giving his mercy to you. Why is it easier for you to give judgement instead of mercy?

7. Jesus uses a bit of humor in verses 41-42, describing our ridiculous attempts to help our brother with a speck in his eye when we have a huge, wooden beam protruding from our own eye, blocking our view. When have you tried to help a fellow believer with a speck in her eye, while avoiding dealing with the log in your own eye?

8. This passage ends with Jesus describing those who don't take his words seriously as a fruitless tree or a house built on an unstable foundation. Stop, pray, and consider in what areas of your life you have resisted following Jesus's words. Write down a prayer of repentance, asking the Spirit to provide the necessary help for you in this area.

Focus verse: *"But love your enemies, and do good, and lend, expecting nothing in return, and your reward will be great, and you will be sons of the Most High, for he is kind to the ungrateful and the evil. Be merciful, even as your Father is merciful."*
Luke 6:35-36

Reflections, curiosities, frustrations:

Study 10

Read Luke 7:1-17

Observation Questions

1. List all the details of the healing of the centurion's servant in verses 1–10.

2. What is the statement Jesus made about the centurion? Was the centurion Jewish?

3. List all the details of the healing of the widow's son in verses 11-17.

Recall that in Luke 6, Jesus was in the middle of what was probably a fairly lengthy sermon. He had been explaining to us what life looks like in the upside-down kingdom, where we consider certain kinds of suffering to be a blessing because of the way Jesus shows us our needs and then meets our needs. He also spoke much about mercy, about giving it to our enemies even in the form of forgiveness and undeserved love. Now in chapter 7, in a pattern that would become characteristic of Jesus's life, he goes out and lives what he taught. Jesus had given his lecture; now he would work it out in the lab. He had just explained in his sermon the culture of the community he was creating; now he would show them what it looked like in day-to-day life. Word, then deed. Teaching, then action. Jesus's ministry always included both.

Verses 1-10. "Centurion" by this point in history was used to refer to a man in charge of between sixty and one hundred soldiers. These were tested, steady officers who made up the backbone of Roman control in first-century Palestine. But unlike the description of most centurions who regularly treated their servants like property, disposing of them like old tools when they were no longer useful, this man was well respected by the Jewish community and treated his servants with dignity. In fact, he had treated the entire establishment of Israel with respect by using his own money to pay for their place of worship. His exact relationship to the God of Israel is not clear in this passage, but as Leon Morris points out, "A man would scarcely have undertaken all that is involved in building a synagogue without some interest in the God who was worshipped there."

Someone in this centurion's life told him about Jesus, the teacher who had been healing in the region. Perhaps it was a servant watching the other servant die who first mentioned Jesus. News was constantly spreading about Jesus's miracles, so it is no surprise that these stories would have eventually reached the household of the centurion. As a man of authority, he would have regularly moved men into action simply by the power of his word, dispatching groups of people to certain places and jobs by sending a messenger here or there with his orders. This centurion approached Jesus in the same way, by sending a group of Jewish elders to request his help. Having been immersed in the culture for some time, the centurion knew to send Jews to the Jew. Notice the elders' argument as to why Jesus should come. The centurion was worthy: "he loves our nation, and he is the one who built us our synagogue" (verse 5). This is usually our heart's assumption, that we deserve for God to do things for us. The centurion knew the truth, that he deserved nothing from Jesus.

But the centurion also would have known something else about Jesus the Jew: coming to the house of a Gentile like himself would have made him ritually unclean. So before Jesus even got to his house, the centurion sent another group of people to stop Jesus and give him a message. As a military officer, the man lived in a strict hierarchy of authority. He had people to whom he answered and people who answered to him. This man had deduced that just like he could send his word and make things happen without even being present, Jesus could do the same. Just as the centurion had authority over scores of men, he understood that Jesus had authority over sickness and death. The centurion, though not given the pedigree and training of the Jews, had figured out that in the chain of command of death and disease, Jesus was at the top. Jesus marveled at his faith. This Gentile understood that Jesus could do anything. And so he did not stumble in his request with unbelief or uncertainty about Jesus's intentions. He knew Jesus was able, so he asked. Is this our approach to Jesus in our need?

Verses 11–17. Again we see Jesus living out his sermon as he enters a town called Nain. Let's set the scene as we attempt to enter the world of this poor, grieving woman. First, this woman was a widow who had lost her only son. At this time and place in history, without some other immediate relative to care for her, her son's death would have sentenced this woman to poverty, with no opportunity to make a living. Piled on top of her heartbreak was the knowledge that she would soon be begging for food and would probably be homeless. Within eight hours of her son's death, because of the inevitable decay of bodies, she and her community would have wrapped her son in strips of cloth and applied spices to distract from the smell of decomposition. Even in her poverty, professional flute players and at least one mourner would have been hired. The son would have been carried either on a plain wooden plank or in a large wicker basket, open to the air and easily seen by those processing and watching the procession. It would have been noisy, the flutes playing a slow, sad dirge and the paid mourners making quite a racket. They would have been making their way from the widow's house to the grave outside the town, where his body was to be placed probably alongside his father's bones.

Enter Jesus. By the time he got near enough to the widow to see her face, he would have known the purpose of the procession. When he saw her, the pain on her face, the tears that wouldn't stop, the heavy weight of grief hanging on her, he had compassion on her. He knew the tightness in his chest and the wet in his eyes that come from from hurting for another. This woman was the poor for whom he had come to proclaim good news; she was the oppressed he had come to liberate (Luke 4:18). He felt compassion, and he did something about it that was unthinkable. He touched the body. No wonder the people carrying the dead man stopped! This was inconceivable for a Jew. Touching a dead body would render a Jew unclean for seven days and would require elaborate cleansing rituals to restore him. But the situation got even stranger. Jesus spoke to the dead man. And just as with the centurion's servant, Jesus's word was enough to "halt the tragic procession to the grave."

What Jesus did next was a thing of mercy and understanding. He could have called the man to come and follow him. This would have been logical, given that Jesus was on a speaking/ministry tour, trying to get the word out about the kingdom. But Jesus had seen, really seen, the man's mother. He knew that sending her son out into some traveling ministry would put her in the very same place he had found her earlier—alone and destitute. And so, acting as the benevolent king that he is, Jesus "gave him to his mother" (verse 15). His calling and place of obedience was to care for this widow. What about us? It is easy to fixate on a call to the glamorous, traveling, exotic ministry, where unknown and interesting challenges await us. Sometimes and for some of us, that is our calling. But often Jesus calls us to faithfulness in the seemingly ordinary things of taking care of our families and serving those nearest us who cannot provide or advocate for themselves.

Of course, the crowds reacted to the healing of the son. They gave God glory and talked about a great prophet and God visiting his people. As usual, there is a story behind their reaction. Read 1 Kings 17. The Jews in the crowd would have known this story. It would have been the story that immediately came to their minds as they watched Jesus raise the son of a widow from the dead. Hence their words about a great prophet; they were equating Jesus with Elijah. "God has visited his people!" they said. They didn't mean that God showed up for a moment to be social; they were using this phrase as the Old Testament writers would have used it: God is blessing his people. He is here to save. Though they did not fully understand who Jesus was, they understood that God was doing something new to save his people, like in Exodus 3, when God told Moses to go and tell the people that he had "visited" them at the burning bush.

These two stories of loss and redemption tell us some things about Jesus. First, Jesus feels deep compassion. The word used for compassion here is the strongest in the Greek language. Compassion is "a feeling of deep sympathy and sorrow for another who is stricken by misfortune, accompanied by a strong desire to alleviate the suffering." This one who knew the glory of humans in their true state of happiness and joy before the Fall certainly felt immense sorrow as he watched them labor to navigate the brokenness of this world. Any sort of empathy we experience for our fellow humans he has felt in a more profound way.

Second, Jesus is a man of both words and action. He's not afraid to get his hands dirty. He doesn't just talk the talk; he walks the walk. He is not some detached deity who guards himself from the mess of our lives. He walks in our dirt, speaks our language, touches our dead, and cries our tears. He knows the implications and heaviness of our losses, and he does something about them. Notice that no one asked him to intervene for the widow. And yet when he confronted such pain, he could not help but act. This is Jesus's compassion, a compassion that heals, reunites loved ones, and reverses death. This is the compassion that would eventually lead him to give himself on a cross in order to do something about all of the pain and loss and grief, to halt the tragic procession to the grave for all who believe in him. In this, the upside-down kingdom, the only one who was ever perfectly clean and sinless would become sin itself so that these terrible places of loss would not be the end of our story. May the reports about him continue to spread, even in our age, even in our regions, even today.

Reflection Questions

4. Jesus extended compassion and healing to a servant of a man, the centurion, who was around the people of God but not one of them. What does this communicate about Jesus's compassion on both his children and those that do not know him yet? What about this has been hard for you to replicate in your own life?

5. The centurion requested that Jesus heal his servant in an unentitled way, not feeling worthy of it but trusting in Jesus's power and authority over all illness. Do you come to Jesus in the same way in regard to healing and illness? Why or why not?

6. Jesus was not asked to heal the widow's son but just looked at her and had such compassion that he did it. What about this compassion surprises you? What about it do you crave?

7. Jesus healed the servant and the widow's son so they could continue in faithfulness in the seemingly ordinary things of taking care of a boss and a widowed mother. What does this show us about the dignity that God gives to the details of our lives?

8. Both of these stories show the Son of God touching, entering in, healing, and being in the pain with his people. What from these accounts of Jesus have you personally experienced in your own life? What parts do you long to experience?

Focus verse: *And when the Lord saw her, he had compassion on her and said to her, "Do not weep." Then he came up and touched the bier, and the bearers stood still. And he said, "Young man, I say to you, arise."*
Luke 7:13-14

Reflections, curiosities, frustrations:

Study 11

The Discouraged Prophet and the Forgiven Woman

Read Luke 7:18-50

Observation Questions

1. Who did John the Baptist send to talk to Jesus? And what was Jesus's response?

2. List some of the statements Jesus said to the crowd after John's disciples left (verses 24-35)?

did you go in the desert to see
a man who could be easily swayed
like a reed in the wind
shaking

3. List the details of what happened when Jesus went to the Pharisee's house for dinner in verses 36-50 (who was there, what they each did, what was said, etc.).

> Cool water to
> Wash their feet
> a Kiss of Peace from the host
> To demonstrat repect
> Smelling oil

Verses 18-30. Before we are too hard on him, we should consider John's circumstances. Recall that a short time after baptizing Jesus, John was put into prison by Herod. He had not been present for Jesus's teaching or miracles. He, like most of Israel, expected the Messiah (the anointed one promised by God in the Old Testament) to set in motion a series of events including armies marching, governments falling, and sure judgment. The reports he was hearing about Jesus included none of the above. Furthermore, this man who had spent years in the vast, open desert was now shut up in a small, stuffy, dark prison. John was confused. And John was discouraged.

As an answer, John's disciples got a front row seat to Jesus healing diseases, plagues, blindness, and exorcising demons. Jesus sent them back to John with a few lines from the Book of Isaiah as an additional clue. Jesus was not about to boldly proclaim his messianic identity in front of crowds and religious leaders; he still had work to do. Instead, he let his actions explain his identity. Jesus was not bringing the kingdom that was expected. He was bringing the kingdom that was. And instead of brute force and coercion, his kingdom would be governed by mercy and love. This was a complete paradigm shift, even for those who had been looking for the Messiah. It was the upside-down kingdom, whose king was walking among immodest prostitutes and arrogant Pharisees. The one who was not offended, who literally was not "trapped" by a false assessment of Jesus, would be blessed. We, too, may be trapped by a false assessment of Jesus, holding onto an idea of him that must be corrected by the real Jesus we meet in his Word.

As John's disciples left, Jesus continued his obvious/not so obvious declaration of his own identity. He asked the crowds, Did you go into the desert to see a man easily swayed like a reed shaking in the wind? Or someone dressed for comfort and an easy life? No. You went to see the dividing line between one era and the next. You saw the forerunner to the Messiah. You saw the last in the age of anticipation, the time of promise. He was great. But anyone in the kingdom is greater than him. As Leon Morris explains, "The least in the kingdom is greater, not because of any personal qualities he may have, but because he belongs to the time of fulfilment." John was still looking forward, pointing to the person everyone had been waiting for—Jesus. Everyone after Jesus, including the saints today, lives in a greater time. The promises have come true; the Messiah has come.

Verses 31–35. Children who spent their days in the open market in Jesus's day would, to amuse themselves, act out scenes of weddings and funerals, the public dramas with which they would have been familiar. They would try to entice others to participate, playing a joyful flute for a wedding enactment or a sad dirge to depict a funeral. When other children refused to play as directed, they complained, accusing them of not being willing to play one way or the other. Jesus's words about his generation were not flattering. He was comparing them to fickle children. No matter how God came to them, they only complained and refused to listen. Neither the self-denying John nor the indulgent Jesus pleased the Pharisees. But, according to verse 35, there would be those who would see God in any approach. The wise people of that day had ears to hear and heard the wisdom of God in both John and Jesus.

Verses 36–50. This woman was no stranger to judgment. Probably a former prostitute, she was used to the condemning looks, the pointing, the whispers. But something had happened that changed the trajectory of her life and redirected her affections. It is unclear from the text whether she had met Jesus in person or had simply heard his teaching. But she had come to understand something of her sinfulness and his saving power. What was she doing in Simon the Pharisee's house? Dinner at a house like Simon's was not the private occasion we experience in our homes. Instead, anyone was free to come and listen to the wisdom taught by the rabbi. Therefore, this woman was free to enter. It was common to have a courtyard in the center of the house where meals would have been served when the weather was pleasant. Guests did not sit in chairs but laid down, usually on their left side. Their right hand was used to eat, and their feet would extend out from the table.

The woman had come with the intention of anointing Jesus's feet with perfume. Many Jewish women wore a small bottle of perfumed oil, expensive and precious. In fact, this oil was probably equivalent to about one year's wages. It was stored in a jar made of stone similar to marble, only softer. These jars had a long neck that was broken off when the oil was used. This woman wanted to express her love and gratitude by giving Jesus the most valuable thing she had. The norm was to pour this type of oil on the head. Pouring it on Jesus's feet was a mark of humility. It is probable that when the woman entered the house to do her task, came near to Jesus, heard his voice, experienced his powerful presence, and began to touch him, she was overcome with emotion. Silent tears began to wet Jesus's feet as the host droned on about whatever amused him. This woman could not contain her gratitude and love for Jesus as she worshipped him, acutely aware of what she owed him.

Simon was having a very different experience. Probably more of a frequent entertainer of celebrities than a spiritual seeker,

Simon sat silently judging both Jesus and the woman. Whatever possibility he had entertained of Jesus being a prophet had died when Jesus let the sinful woman touch him. But Jesus, as usual when it comes to knowing the hearts of men, was ten steps ahead of Simon.

When guests came to dinner in first-century Palestine, common courtesy dictated several things. First, cool water would have been given to wash their dry, dirty feet. A kiss of peace from the host to the guests would have demonstrated respect. Finally, some sort of good smelling oil or other substance was placed on the guests' heads. Simon had done none of these things for Jesus. His invitation had the appearance of respect, but was actually insulting. Jesus, of course, knew this. So while Simon self-righteously wrote off both Jesus and the woman, Jesus told a story that cut straight through his smug, arrogant attitude.

Notice that Jesus is "answering" Simon's thoughts. Simon hadn't actually said anything, but more than just knowing exactly who the woman was, Jesus knew exactly who Simon was. And so he told him a story. Jesus craftily wove a parable that identified both Simon and the woman as debtors. What's the difference between them? The woman knew how much she owed. She understood that because of her many sins, she owed God a tremendous amount. And she could not pay. Just as the debtor in the story, the woman's debt of sin had been cancelled by Jesus. Her response? Complete and total adoration. Overflowing gratitude and love for the one who had so graciously cancelled the debt she legitimately owed. And Simon? Simon thought he could pay. Pharisees didn't think they were sinless, but they thought their good deeds could balance out their bad ones. Simon thought that by keeping the law he could pay back his debt. He didn't know his need for help outside of himself. He thought he was a "good person." He believed his goodness was all that was required. This is an extremely dangerous belief.

Once again, Jesus was living out in practice his own great sermon of the previous chapter. He was showing everyone what the upside-down kingdom looked like. While everyone else would have honored Simon for his status and good practices, Jesus honored the woman for her need and submission. While Simon judged the woman and wrote her off, Jesus elevated her and forgave her sins. While the Pharisees relied on their own strength, actions, and practice, Jesus praised the unclean, scandalous woman. Why? Because she knew how sinful she was, and she knew how much she needed Jesus's forgiveness. This is what elevates those in the kingdom—not their own rightness, but Jesus's righteousness; not their accomplishments, but Jesus's sinless life; not their own reputations, but Jesus's. All we need to know to enter this beautiful upside-down kingdom is the magnitude of our debt and Jesus's mercy.

Reflection Questions

4. Discouragement had taken hold of even the great John the Baptist as he sat in his prison cell, leading him to send for answers from Jesus. When you feel discouraged or confused by how a situation has turned out, to whom do you turn for insight and help? What is most helpful to you to change your perspective?

5. In the text Jesus compares the people to fickle children, since no matter what form God was bringing his kingdom they were not pleased with it. Around what issues in your own life do you see this in your response to God? Why?

6. The "sinful woman" in the passage knew her high need and felt the greatness of her weakness, resulting in her faith and demonstration of love toward Jesus. What weaknesses in your personal story draw you near to Jesus like this? Explain.

7. Simon the Pharisee had judgement for such a needy display by the woman, thinking he was capable to do enough good to cross out his bad, without needing Jesus. Where currently in your life are you functioning like Simon? Of what do you need to repent?

8. In this scene at Simon's house we see two very different reactions to the same Jesus. Why do you think that is? Of the two which reaction does your heart more regularly have to him? Why?

9. Jesus's response to the woman's act of washing his feet was to say, "Your faith has saved you; go in peace," demonstrating that faith saved her, but it resulted in an expression of works. What about the tension between justification by faith alone and good works as the fruit of faith is confusing to you? Where has your faith lead you to outward action?

Focus verse: *Therefore I tell you, her sins, which are many, are forgiven —for she loved much. But he who is forgiven little, loves little. And he said to her, "Your sins are forgiven."*
Luke 7:47-48

Reflections, curiosities, frustrations:

Study 12

Rocky Soil and a Storm

Read Luke 8:1-25

Observation Questions

1. Who are the people who had been traveling with Jesus? List their names and what the text tells us about them (verses 1-3).

discuples

2. List the different types of soil and what they each represent in the parable of the sower (verses 4-15).

3. List the details of what happened when Jesus and his disciples got caught in a storm on the lake in verses 22–25 (who was there, what they each did, what was said, etc.).

Verses 1–3. Jesus was no longer teaching in synagogues. The crowds were now large and came from long distances to hear him. He continued on a preaching tour in the region of Galilee with his disciples. But along with this band of men was another small crowd: a group of wealthy women. It was not unusual for cult leaders, psychics, or other traveling men in the ancient world to have female benefactors. But these women were not just giving their money; they were traveling with and serving Jesus. Mary Magdalene had previously been inhabited by seven demons, and Jesus had released her from their grip. Joanna was married to Herod's so-called chief of staff, the manager of all of his affairs, and Jesus had healed her of some sickness. These women, like the woman who came to Simon's house to anoint Jesus's feet with oil in the previous chapter, loved Jesus. He had healed them of terrible afflictions. Out of their gratefulness, they provided for his physical needs and became his traveling companions. According to the feminine version of "who" in verse 3, there were many other women as well. While the rabbis refused to teach women, considering them inferior, Jesus included them as vital parts of the community that served and ministered with him.

Verses 4–15. The parable of the sower is the first parable found in Matthew, Mark, and Luke (Matthew 14, Mark 4). It is the parable that sets the paradigm for understanding the kingdom. A simple definition of a parable is a story that makes a point. But these little stories are so much more than that. They are indirect communication. They are stories with intent. They are "allusive narrative which is told for an ulterior purpose." Most of them are stories with not one but two levels of meaning: an obvious meaning and a not-so-obvious, hidden meaning. They are "expanded analog[ies] used to convince and persuade." Why did Jesus talk like this? Why did he tell stories that were less than straightforward?

Consider the crowds that were listening to Jesus at this point. They were enormous. And they were mixed. In these crowds were genuine seekers of the coming Messiah. Though they may or may not have known the Old Testament Scriptures that described God's anointed one who was to come, they knew their need. They were listening, waiting, and looking for deliverance. Also in the crowd were people who wanted to align themselves with the next military leader. There were those who thought Jesus might be the next political power. There were many who were afflicted with diseases or demon possession who wanted healing. There were those casually going along with the crowds and those who simply came to see what the fuss was all about. This mass of humanity with mixed motives came to listen to Jesus. Parables were the method he used to distinguish the genuine seekers from the thousands of others. All four types of "soil" would have been present and represented in the large crowd to which he was speaking.

The "secrets" Jesus mentions in verse 9 are not secret knowledge unknowable by humans. Jesus is referring to an understanding of the kingdom that must be revealed by God himself. God had given the disciples and some in the crowds comprehension and perception of Jesus's teaching. But concerning the others, he quoted Isaiah 6:9-10, where God commissioned Isaiah to go and preach saying, "Go, and say to this people: 'Keep on hearing, but do not understand; keep on seeing, but do not perceive.' Make the heart of this people dull, and their ears heavy, and blind their eyes; lest they see with their eyes, and hear with their ears, and understand with their hearts, and turn and be healed." Just as Isaiah was to speak to hard-hearted Israel, Jesus speaks in parables as a form of prophetic warning to those who do not believe. There would be judgment for some. Not all of the listeners were the same. Jesus laid out the meaning of the parable for his disciples. The seed is God's Word, and it is the condition of the soil that matters. In the first soil, the seed of the Word of God never even takes root. In the second, it blooms for a bit and then dies when tested. In the third, with the passing of time, the enthusiastic commitment that was first made is squeezed out by all of the other cares of this world. Only the good soil eventually bears fruit. And it bears a miraculous yield—one hundredfold. The regular expectation for the yield of a cereal crop would have been four- to fivefold. God's Word in rich soil has far greater yields. What was the fruit borne by the good soil? Obedience to God's Word over the long haul. Discipleship with perseverance. Not perfect discipleship, but a fruit-bearing life. As C. Kenner observes, "The only conversions that count in the kingdom are those confirmed by a life of discipleship."

Verses 16–21. The description Jesus gives of the lamp continues the theme of the sower. Once the message has been heard, the genuine believer bears fruit as she reveals that message to others, like a light on a stand for others to see. Verse 18 encourages us again to be rich soil: "Take care then how you hear." Jesus's followers needed to be, as we still need to be, attentive in how we listen to his Word. How we listen and our receptivity to the teaching he has already given us determines whether or not he chooses to reveal more to us by his power. As Leon Morris explains, "If we use what God gives it will increase… if we do not, we will lose even what we think we have."

Jesus's mother and brothers had had interesting interactions and doubts about Jesus before this short scene in verses 19-21. In Mark 3:21 we read they literally thought he was out of his mind. It may seem that Jesus was denying his family or being cruel to them, especially in his culture, where family meant everything. But Jesus was not telling us he didn't love his family. He was showing us that God's kingdom came before everything else. Obedience to God's Word was Jesus's first priority. Those who shared this belief were even closer to him than his earthly family.

Verses 22-25. The lake where this storm took place sits six hundred feet below sea level. It is surrounded by mountainous regions with giant ravines, through which cold air from the mountains rushes down toward the lake, generating sudden, violent storms. Notice it is Jesus who led these disciples to the storm. Some of these men were fishermen, well versed in lake travel. They had seen a storm or two. But this storm scared them. Jesus, having taught probably most of the day, was tired. He was human and exhausted, and while the storm raged and water began to fill the boat, he slept on. The disciples had seen enough of Jesus to know they needed him. But they clearly had not yet comprehended his entire identity. They woke him in full panic mode. "We are perishing!" they said. But the real fear came for the disciples as they saw what Jesus did next. Just over the crashing of the waves, the whipping wind, and the shouts among themselves, they heard Jesus rebuke the elements. And it was calm. Just like that. The word of this man, Jesus, had stopped the violent storm. Then the real fear started, as they considered the power not of the storm but of the one standing in their boat.

"Who then is this?" they asked each other. This is the central question of Luke. Who is this man? Is he Messiah? The anointed one to come? But we thought he would come and overthrow the government with his power. We thought he would lead an army that trampled every other. We expected political power plays. We thought we would see decisive condemnation of all but the Jews. This Jesus is not doing any of these things. But he is the one who heals diseases, exorcises demons, and raises widows' sons from the dead like Elijah. He tells stories that make it harder to follow him, not easier. He puts obedience to God even above loyalty to family. And the wind and waves listen to his word.

He may not be who we or the disciples were expecting, but he is someone we cannot ignore. We, like the first hearers of Jesus's words, must "take care then how [we] hear." The king of the upside-down kingdom is giving his Word to those who have ears to hear. May we be the good, rich soil, ready for the seed.

Reflection Questions

4. What do you find interesting or surprising about the list of women traveling with Jesus? Why?

They had money, also Jesus
healed them, mary madaleen
was healed from the demans
releled her from her grip
they

they take care of
Jesus Needs
i noyit his feet

5. What did you learn about parables, one of Jesus main forms of teaching, that you didn't know before? What is your reaction to Jesus's use of them to expose those who want to follow him and those who don't? for the Pefole that don't belive

Parables, a story that makes a point
stores of 2 levels, obvious meaning
and not so obvious
Seekers of the messiha from
the politions and political
power

6. In the list of descriptions about the soils, which one have you seen occur most often in your own life or the life of others around you? Which description was confusing? What would you like to understand better? hearing, but don't understand
peple you
condishtion of the soil

7. Jesus's reaction to his family demonstrates how much the body of believers are a true family in a unique way and often to a greater degree than our family of origin. Have you found this to be true in your own life? Explain. *yes*

8. In the storm on the boat the disciples went from ordering Jesus to save them to fearing him when he was able to quiet the storm with his words. When have you experienced a similar shift in your own relationship with God—going from demanding things from him to awe and respect for his power and authority?

when the storm is quit, you still can speak to Hr and have respect

Focus verse: *And they went and woke him, saying, "Master, Master, we are perishing!" And he awoke and rebuked the wind and the raging waves, and they ceased, and there was a calm. He said to them, "Where is your faith?" And they were afraid, and they marveled, saying to one another, "Who then is this, that he commands even winds and water, and they obey him?"*
Luke 8:24-25

Reflections, curiosities, frustrations:

Study 13

Demon Possession and the Bleeding Woman

Read Luke 8:26-56

Observation Questions

1. Describe the details of what happened when Jesus healed the demon-possessed man in verses 26–39 (who was there, what they each did, what was said, etc.). the demon went into the pigs, they ran down to the water and drond

2. Where did the woman touch Jesus when he was on his way to heal the little girl? What do we know about this woman?

3. List the details of what happened when Jesus healed Jairus's daughter in verses 49–56 (who was there, what they each did, what was said, etc.).

Verses 26–39. Jesus and his disciples had come out of the storm and into Gentile (not Jewish) territory. They had barely been on land when the poor, tortured man housing many demons met them. See the horror Satan had worked in this man's life. He had been stripped of his dignity, isolated, physically harmed, violent. He was alone, and no one could do anything to help. It had been this way for "a long time." It was not even the man who addressed Jesus, but the demons. Notice that they quickly and clearly answered the question the disciples had asked in the boat. Who was Jesus? Jesus was the Son of the Most High God. Satan called him this not to worship him but as a matter of fact. And then he did something remarkable. He begged Jesus for mercy. Why?

The devil has a false reputation. Many of us have been taught that Jesus and Satan are in some kind of never-ending war, with plot twists and a balance of power that will one day crescendo to an unpredictable battle for the world. This is incorrect. The war is real, to be sure, but the outcome is already known. Jesus wins, and Satan knows it. He may pester and hassle God's children while on earth, but when faced with God head-on, all his minions can do is beg. In order to do anything, they must have Jesus's permission. We don't know if Jesus was asking the man's name or the demon's, but it was the demon(s) who answered. A "legion" was a regiment of six thousand soldiers. Many demons had dominated this man, holding him hostage. The demons knew Jesus could do what he wanted with them. They only hoped he would not send them into the Abyss, a place where spirits were confined and that was understood to be boundless and bottomless. The demons continued to beg, until Jesus gave them permission to enter the pigs. Just as the wind and waves had to obey Jesus's word, so did the demons.

Notice how the people of the region reacted in fear just like the disciples did when Jesus calmed the storm. These are not silly little stories. These were real people who saw supernatural things happen, unexplainable by human power. But this was where the people of the region made their mistake. Instead of welcoming the one who set their fellow human free, they asked him to leave. They may have valued the pigs more than the man who had been tortured. They may have not liked their lives being disturbed. Whatever the reason, Jesus's ministry in the region of the Gerasenes was over.

The freed man's ministry, however, was just beginning. Of course he wanted to stay near Jesus. His love and gratitude probably equaled that of the others Jesus had healed. But Jesus's call to the man was this: "Return home and tell how much God has done for you." He sent the man back home to his family, friends, and villagers to tell his story. Jesus had been very careful on the other side of the lake not to directly declare his identity. But for this Gentile man, freed from the torture of Satan, he laid it out plainly. What he, Jesus, had done was what God had done.

Verses 40-56. Jesus's display of power and authority was not over. He returned from his trip across the lake to a waiting crowd. From within the crowd came Jairus, a ruler of the synagogue. He would have been a man of some prestige, someone who chose the readers of Scriptures and leaders of prayer on the Sabbath. But this was his only daughter, and she was dying. Her age, twelve, signified that she was just on the verge of womanhood in her culture, maybe even contemplating marriage. Her distinguished father humbled himself before Jesus, got on his knees, and begged. Like the demons, like the man who had been healed, this father came in desperation. In moments of real need, there is no better place to be than begging before Jesus.

Meanwhile, a woman was sneaking through the crowd. According to Jewish ceremonial law, she was unclean. She had been bleeding for twelve years, probably with some sort of gynecological problem. Any self-respecting Jewish rabbi would not let a bleeding woman touch him. She knew this and had probably been living an isolated life along with physical pain. She stealthily worked her way to Jesus, believing if she could just touch him she had a chance of being healed. It was a crowded street, as most of the streets in that area and that time were very narrow. Think of working your way toward a concession stand at a packed football game or a busy concert. People were pressed up against each other, trying to see, to get through, to ask Jesus for something.

Suddenly Jesus felt something. The woman had probably touched the tassel that was attached to the corner of the garment Jesus was wearing. This portion of square cloth was traditionally thrown over the left shoulder and hung down the back, reachable without the wearer's knowledge. Immediately she was healed. But Jesus would not let her slip away in the same way she had snuck toward him. He began calling her out, not because he didn't know who she was or what had happened, but because he wanted to expose her. Why would he do such a thing? Think back to the leper in Luke 5. Jesus healed him physically, but he knew the leper needed to be restored to his community as well, so he commanded him to go show the priest so that everyone would know he was clean and could resume a social and productive life. This woman was physically healed, but she needed more than that and Jesus knew it. She needed to be restored to community and freedom. Jesus made her testify to her cleanliness in front of everyone. Not only that, he dignified her by calling her daughter and sending her away in peace, just as he had the sinful woman who wet his feet with her tears. Far from being secondary or patronized by Jesus, the women he met were honored, called to service, and treated with respect.

Back to Jairus's daughter. It was too late; she was dead. Or so it seemed. Jesus reassured the distraught father, requiring him to "only believe." All of the emotion must have swept over the father as he entered the house. There were the mourners, the wailing women, the crying mother. There was his only daughter, lying motionless on her deathbed. Jesus touched her. This was the second time in the span of only a few minutes that he had become unclean. According to Jewish law, touching a dead body was even worse than touching a bleeding woman. But, Jesus was about to make the girl clean. The power of Jesus and his word was again on display: "Child, arise." In that moment, the spirit that had left her young body returned. Jesus, never neglecting the details and everyday needs of people around him, told them to give her something to eat.

As he had done over and over, he told the parents to keep quiet about what had happened. He often tried to avoid publicity. He was not yet ready to make a public declaration of his identity. But those around him were seeing the power of God through Jesus. The disciples had heard him explain the kingdom in the lecture, then watched him heal and touch and set people free in the lab. His power was on display everywhere he went. He had raised multiple people from the dead, cast out demons, and calmed a storm. All of this he did with his word. He did not conjure up someone else's name or authority. He only needed to speak for things to happen.

We have traced the life of Jesus from his birth in a dirty cave. Born to a powerless, teenage mother, foretold by a miracle child born to two elderly people, and raised in a poor family, Jesus lived a difficult life in our broken world. From the very beginning, he had chosen to deal with the suffering of humanity by entering into it. He endured the testing of Satan in the wilderness and the rejection of the religious leaders. He called a band of unlikely disciples and began a preaching tour complete with demonstrations of God's power. He withdrew to pray when he could have rallied for insurrection. He taught love for enemies when he alone had the right to condemn. He saw and had compassion on those who were hurting, released people from the tortures of Satan, and called an unclean woman "daughter." Who was this man? Who is this man? He is the Son of the Most High God, the anointed one who was to come, the Messiah, the king of the upside-down kingdom. And to those who put their trust in him, he still says, "Your faith has made you well. Go in peace."

Reflection Questions

4. Jesus's healing of the demon-possessed man exposes to us the battle going on in the spiritual realm that we often do not see. What about that makes you uncomfortable or confused?

5. The people who witnessed the healing of the demon-possessed man were filled with fear and wanted him to leave their town. When have you witnessed an act of God or learned something of his power and it felt scary? Why?

6. The desperate, bleeding woman needed not only to be healed but also to be restored to community. Why is being in community so crucial for emotional and spiritual health?

7. All that was needed to heal Jairus's daughter was Jesus's word, but he used touch also. What does this teach us about God's desire to enter in physical, present ways? How does that convict you?

8. Twice in this passage we see Jesus not only fulfilling the law but mercifully doing what the law could not do by healing the bleeding woman and the dead daughter. What is your reaction to Jesus's merciful actions? Describe a recent circumstance where you either extended mercy or it was extended to you.

9. Write at least three takeaways from the first eight chapters of Luke.

Focus verse: *And when the woman saw that she was not hidden, she came trembling, and falling down before him declared in the presence of all the people why she had touched him, and how she had been immediately healed. And he said to her, "Daughter, your faith has made you well; go in peace."*
Luke 8:47–48

Reflections, curiosities, frustrations:

Acknowledgments

Hope: To Ray, thank you for loving me well everyday, making me laugh, and pushing me to try. To my children, Cana, Thea, and Nias, love you guys so much; thanks for being you and just fun to be around. To my parents, thank you for giving me unconditional love, support, and your presence. TCU Sisters, your cheerleading and "speaking in" has been path altering this year. Kelly Buck, thanks for reminding me of what I really am even if it is scary. Hunter Beless, our social marketing coach, you have been the greatest gift and highlight of this whole process this time around! Renae and Jacob, you are two of the best people we could have on our team, and you both so selflessly serve us and our million questions—thank you! Chris, can you belive we get to do this still? And may we always bring glory and honor to his name.

Chris: Michael, I hope you know that no books would have been written without you. And I don't just mean your helpful opinions, wise suggestions, marketing ideas, risk-taking nature, and networking experience. I mean that you believe in me, and did so long before I did. You trusted me with ideas, people, and your own heart when my track record deserved none of the above. You are my first and favorite consultant. And the cutest. Betty, you are an unexpected gift from the Lord. Hunter, you have done more for us than you're willing to acknowledge. I'm so thankful to have you as a trusted ally. Jen Hinrichs, I'm pretty sure I don't deserve your encouragement and loyalty, but I'm so thankful for you! Mollie and Melanie, I could not have survived this season without your very particular and practical help. Andi, your words of encouragement about my writing have helped me believe I could do this. Renae, you deserved the margarita by the Riverwalk; thank you for being excellent. Jacob, thank you for being such a gentle leader for us.

A Note on Sources

I have drawn from a wealth of other people's hard work in my study of Luke. I am first indebted to Dr. Dan Doriani, who taught Gospels at Covenant Seminary with such excellence and who also directed me to specific commentators to be trusted in their treatment of the text. I have relied on biblehub.com for their excellent Greek interlinear verses and their commentators, specifically Clarke and Ellicott. I have used monergism.com multiple times to access sermons, especially those of Sinclair Ferguson and Alistair Begg. I have also consulted Bruce J. Malina's *The New Testament World, Insights from Cultural Anthropology* (Westminster/John Knox Press, 1993). What a wonderful resource for understanding the world in which Jesus lived.

Notes

2. Angels and the Impossible: Luke 1:1–38

11   Zechariah may have given up praying for a child: Liefeld and Pao, "Luke," 54.

12   In Ephesians 1:6: Ibid., 60.

12   "apart from any merit": Ibid.

3. Songs and Prophecy Fulfilled: Luke 1:39–80

17   Leon Morris describes this section: Morris, *Luke*, 93.

17   "It is not the proud or the mighty": Ibid., 94.

18   Here, a "horn of salvation": Liefeld and Pao, "Luke," 70.

4. Angels, Shepherds, and Temple Visits: Luke 2:1–52

24   Augustus was taking a census: Ibid., 75.

24   He changed the Roman republic into an empire: Ibid., 78.

24   "We do not know": Morris, *Luke*, 101.

25   This, the offering Mary and Joseph brought: Ibid., 104.

5. John and Jesus: Luke 3:1–38

33   "Repentance throws into reverse gear": Ferguson, "Voice in the Wilderness."

33   According to a rabbinic saying: Morris, *Luke*, 114.

6. Satan's Temptations and Jesus's Authority: Luke 4:1-44

39   In that year, according to Leviticus 25: Liefeld and Pao, "Luke," 105.

40   Apparently a holy war had been launched: Ibid., 111.

41   It was a politically tense time: Morris, *Luke*, 131.

7. The New Disciples and Unexpected Healings: Luke 5:1-39

47   "The psychological effects of all this": Ibid., 135.

48   "As a class they were regarded": Ibid., 139.

48   "Fasting reflects a condition of dissatisfaction": Liefeld and Pao, 127.

8. Upside-Down Blessing: Luke 6:1-26

52   "Ceremonial rites (being only means to an end)": Ibid., 129.

55   "Blessed" here means: Keller, "Community."

56   "'Woe to you' is an expression": Morris, *Luke*, 148.

56   "Together with the ... woes": Ibid., 146.

9. Enemies, Judging Others, and Fruitlessness: Luke 6:27-49

60   "Once again it is the spirit of the saying": Ibid., 150.

61   Jesus is telling us: Ibid., 149.

62   "Almost all ancient nations wore": Clarke, Commentary on Luke 6:38.

10. Healing and Compassion: Luke 7:1–17

69   "A man would scarcely have undertaken": Morris, *Luke*, 156.

71   "halt the tragic procession": Begg, "Compassion of Christ."

72   "a feeling of deep sympathy": Dictionary.com, s.v., "compassion," accessed January 14, 2019, https://www.dictionary.com/browse/compassion.

11. The Discouraged Prophet and the Forgiven Woman: Luke 7:18–50

77   "The least in the kingdom is greater": Morris, *Luke*, 163.

78   Many Jewish women wore a small bottle: Ibid., 166.

12. Rocky Soil and a Storm: Luke 8:1–25

87   They are "allusive narrative": Snodgrass, *Stories with Intent*, 8 (quoting Hans Dieter Betz).

87   They are "expanded analog[ies]": Ibid., 9.

88   "The only conversions that count": Morris, *Luke*, 176 (quoting C. Kenner).

88   "If we use what God gives": Ibid., 171.

Works Cited

Begg, Alistair. "The Compassion of Christ: Luke 7:1–17." Sermon, October 31, 1999. https://www.truthforlife.org/resources/sermon/the-compassion-of-christ/.

Clarke, Adam. Commentary on Luke 6:38 in *Clarke's Commentary on the Whole Bible*. https://www.biblehub.com/commentaries/clarke/luke/6.htm.

Ferguson, Sinclair. "The Voice in the Wilderness: Luke 3:1–14." Sermon, First Presbyterian Church, Columbia, SC. https://www.monergism.com/legacy/mt/mp3/71-part-sermon-series-gospel-according-luke-dr-sinclair-b-ferguson.

Keller, Tim. "Community Part 1: The Community of Jesus: Luke 6:12–36." Sermon, January 19, 2003. https://gospelinlife.com/?fwp_categories=sermons-talks&fwp_bible=luke-6.

Liefeld, Walter L., and David W. Pao. "Luke." In *Luke–Acts*. Vol. 10 of *The Expositor's Bible Commentary*, rev. ed., edited by Tremper Longman III and David E. Garland. Grand Rapids, MI: Zondervan, 2006.

Morris, Leon. *Luke*. Tyndale New Testament Commentaries. Downers Grove, IL: Intervarsity Press, 1974.

Snodgrass, Klyne. *Stories with Intent: A Comprehensive Guide to the Parables of Jesus*. Grand Rapids, MI: William B. Eerdmans, 2008.

Other At His Feet Studies

We pray that you will continue to sit at the feet of Jesus, studying his word. To help you with this, we have also written Bible studies for women on these books of the Bible:

Romans (28 studies)

1 Samuel (16 studies)

Philippians (12 studies)

Psalms (13 studies)

Made in United States
North Haven, CT
17 January 2023

31149067R00075